you&your
Mitsubishi
Evo

you & your
Mitsubishi
Evo

Andy Butler   *Buying, enjoying, maintaining, modifying*

British Library cataloguing-in-publication data:
A catalogue record for this book is available from the British Library.

Published by Haynes Publishing,
Sparkford, Yeovil, Somerset BA22 7JJ
Tel: 01963 442030 Fax: 01963 440001
Int. tel: +44 1963 442030 Int fax: +44 1963 440001
E-mail: sales@haynes.co.uk
Website: www.haynes.co.uk

ISBN 1 85960 961 9

Library of Congress catalog card number 2003110494

Haynes North America Inc.
861 Lawrence Drive, Newbury Park,
California 91320, USA

Page layout by Glad Stockdale
Printed and bound by in Britain by J.H. Haynes & Co. Ltd,
Sparkford

DEDICATION

This book is dedicated to my wife Zoë, who not only had to live and breathe Mitsubishi when there were probably other things she could have been doing, but who kept me going when it seemed everything was conspiring against me ever getting this finished. I couldn't have done it without you.

Notes on imperial/metric conversions

Unless usually referred to in metric units (eg engine capacity in cubic centimetres [cc] or litres) or imperial units (eg carburettors in inches [in]), common measurements are given in either imperial or metric units as circumstances dictate with their equivalents in parentheses, except in the following less common instances:

$$282 \div \text{miles per gallon (mpg)}$$
$$= \text{litres per 100 kilometres (1/100km)}$$
Torque: pounds-force feet (lb/ft) x 0.113
$$= \text{Newton metres (Nm)}$$
Pressure: pounds-force per square inch (psi)
$$= \text{kilopascals (kPa)}$$

Jurisdictions which have strict emission control laws may consider any modification to a vehicle to be an infringement of those laws. You are advised to check with the appropriate body or authority whether your proposed modification complies fully with the law. The publishers accept no liability in this regard.

While every effort is taken to ensure the accuracy of the information given in this book, no liability can be accepted by the author or publishers for any loss, damage or injury caused by misuse of, errors in, or omissions from, the information given.

Contents

Acknowledgements

This is the bit where I get to thank everyone who made this project come together and work like the finely-tuned machine you'd expect. Or in this case, those people who didn't mind me bombarding them with daft questions and impossible requests with hardly any notice!

At Mitsubishi's Press Office I have to thank Gabi Whitfield and Kelly Archer for finding out what Evo history was available in English – which was not a lot on the early stuff, but we got round that. They also managed to get an Evolution VIII FQ-300 to me when the car had only just been released and motoring journos the length and breadth of the country were screaming to be let loose in one. Ta very much. The book would have looked silly without the VIII's inclusion.

Jim Blackstock from Ralliart Europe got hold of some old motorsport shots that Japan had tucked away in their archives and thought no one would need to see again.

Big thanks to Trevor Mudd of the Mitsubishi Lancer Register for all his help, and to Tony Crossley who is their Evo I–III man. I shamelessly cribbed info from his Lancer Club website buying guide to make sure you know what to look for if you're contemplating buying such a beast. He also owns the Evo I we shot for inclusion here, and didn't mind us pawing all over it.

Clive, Jenny, Max, Paul, Andy, and Lee, at RC Developments in Barnton, let us get in the way in their workshop, stockroom and on the phone, checking and photographing all things Evo. Also, thanks to Max for the wildest ride I've ever had round Oulton Park, finishing up with a two-wheeled 'moment' coming onto the start/finish straight that was so exciting it only seemed scary when we saw everyone else's faces afterwards...

Warrenders in Barnton cleaned up the Evo IV so that we could snap a few piccies of it at short notice, and let us loose in an Evo VII for more pics and more driving entertainment.

Thanks too to Martin Vincent, editor of *Japanese Performance* magazine, not only for getting the photos we needed out of the archive and back to us for use here, but also for editing the mag that lets us go and play in the hairiest and most powerful cars in the country and get paid for doing it.

Thanks also go to Geoff Bullock (Evo II), Steve Law (Evo III), and Dave Mansfield (Evo V) for letting us photograph their Evolutions specially for these pages. Thanks to all the Mitsubishi Evo enthusiasts who run websites worldwide. I've spent many hours scouring these for the early historical information that was hard to find.

I'd also like to thank Mark Hughes and Steve Rendle at Haynes Publishing for letting me loose on this project in the first place, and then allowing me to shift the deadline by several months to include the Evo VIII pics and words, without getting too stressed about it. Sorry!

Finally, I have to thank my wife Zoë Harrison for taking all the photos – apart from the very few that are credited otherwise – as well as encouraging me to keep going when it seemed no one could tell me what I needed to know. She also helped by going through the finished manuscript and pointing out where all the mistakes and inconsistencies were. Thanks for the help, and I hope I've sorted everything that was wrong. If there are any mistakes, they're all mine.

And *really* finally, thanks to Mitsubishi's motorsport-mad engineers, who put the whole Lancer Evolution project together in the first place. Without you guys this would be a very short and uninteresting book.

Andy Butler
Appleby
June 2003

Introduction

Welcome to Mitsubishi world

My first real contact with the Mitsubishi Evolution came about at a 'Run What Ya Brung' drag race event where we were scouting for possible magazine-feature cars. Obviously I'd seen their antics on various rally reports over several seasons, but I'd never actually seen one of the early cars right up close. I spent some hours watching everything from tweaked Minis to monster Yank tanks ripping down the strip as quickly as they could. It was a fun morning.

Then, on a wander through the line of cars waiting to run, I found a Mitsubishi Evolution II. The owner was listening to the stereo, his crash helmet on the passenger seat, and he was looking pretty calm. We had a quick chat about the spec of the car before he had to run up to the line and get staged. It turned out that the car had been treated to a few engine mods, like a performance air filter and an exhaust system, but nothing outlandish. So, mildly interested to see what this almost-standard car would do, I watched him run.

The first intriguing thing we noted was the way he carefully drove around the burnout box and straight up to the start-line. Instead of the macho burnout – obviously a difficult proposition in a permanent four-wheel-drive car – he just ran up to the lights and waited for his opponent to arrive. I can't remember what he was running against, but it was pretty big and built just for drag racing. Whatever, it didn't matter. The lights dropped to green, the Evo catapulted off the line, and 13.6 seconds later it had whupped the other car. It was so impressive because it wasn't impressive. There was no drama, no histrionics. The car just gripped and went. Once I'd seen that I knew that Evos were a bit special, and I've been scribbling about them ever since.

But where did Evos come from, and how did a company like Mitsubishi end up making such a devastatingly effective road and rally weapon? Well, going back in the company's 130-plus year history, there's very little to suggest that it would one day produce such a car. But Mitsubishi has been successful in almost every aspect of its many business ventures, so it should come as no surprise that, having set its corporate mind to achieve such a goal, it should succeed so completely.

Obviously, when the company was first formed in 1870 there were no cars around, and its first successes were in the shipping business. Founder Yatoro Iwasaki changed the firm's name from Tsukomo Shokai to Mitsubishi Shokai in 1873. A far-sighted entrepreneur, Iwasaki ploughed the profits of the shipping operation into diversification rather than more ships, buying land, mining rights, railways, and financial institutions.

By 1900, Mitsubishi-sha Limited was producing large ocean-going vessels that were as good as anything available worldwide, and because of this the Japanese navy started using the home-grown product rather than buying ships from UK yards. This helped make Mitsubishi-sha Limited even bigger and more profitable. The Mitsubishi Shipbuilding Company Limited was registered in 1917, by which time the founder's nephew Koyata Iwasaki had taken over the reins as president. He was every bit as switched on as his uncle, and the company's growth and diversification continued under his control.

While Mitsubishi was dealing with bigger projects, a newfangled machine had arrived from abroad which looked as if it might become quite useful. Although Japan

DID YOU KNOW?

The name Mitsubishi literally means 'three diamonds', and the red triangular logo we know today was based on founder Yatoro Iwasaki's own family crest.

was a few years behind Europe and the USA in developing its own motor cars on a large scale, a small number of vehicles had been put together by engineers who saw how influential the new form of transport could be.

The first Japanese petrol-engined car was made in 1907, but borrowed French chassis technology; some also had American powerplants. Still, the industry had to start somewhere and, as we know today, a mighty oak has grown from that tiniest of acorns. The first car was the Yoshida Type 3, and it was the product of Shintaro Yoshida. He developed cars under the name of the Tokyo Automobile Works, which turned out its first four-cylinder vehicle in 1911.

As the business of motor car production slowly grew Mitsubishi got involved, and in 1917 brought out its wittily-titled Type A. This was made in the company's Kobe shipyard, and was based upon a 1.8-litre Fiat four-cylinder design. However, only a small number of cars were ever produced, and then the whole idea of Mitsubishi making cars was officially scrapped.

Then in 1920 the Mitsubishi Internal Combustion Engine Manufacturing Company Limited was formed. This wasn't just interested in producing engines for cars, though, and in the face of very stiff opposition from the American vehicle manufacturers it looked to other areas to develop its products. Having produced its first aeroplane engine in 1919, Mitsubishi saw the military market as a dependable one that was worth getting into. In fact, it specialised so heavily in this sort of powerplant that in 1928 this subsidiary company's name was changed to the Mitsubishi Aircraft Company Limited.

By the mid-1930s the Japanese government was looking to improve and develop its military strength, and one of the by-products of this was the passing of a law that effectively ended overseas competition within Japan. Both Ford and General Motors had factories in the country, but within a couple of years of the Motorcar Manufacturing Enterprise law coming into effect they had packed up and gone home.

While it might seem strange that Mitsubishi didn't return to the passenger car sector, even though the competition had effectively been removed from the marketplace, they had been working on commercial air transport instead. Through their contacts with the aviation industry, they had branched out from engine production into full aeroplane design and manufacturing. The best known product of this new business was a small single-engined fighter subsequently known as the Zero, which made its maiden flight in 1939. In fact, the Zero was such a successful

design that another company, the Nakajima Aircraft Company Limited, shared in its production so that more fighters could be produced in a shorter time. Interestingly, Nakajima built almost twice as many Zeros as Mitsubishi.

One of the outcomes of American involvement in post-war Japan was that the country's large corporations were split up. Mitsubishi itself was divided into three much smaller parts, and it wasn't until 1964 that they had the chance to reform into Mitsubishi Heavy Industries Limited. During the intervening years Mitsubishi looked to an American motor manufacturer, Kaiser-Frazer, to collaborate in producing US-designed vehicles for the Japanese domestic market. This was a common enough practice, and Nissan, Hino, and Isuzu were all doing similar things. Only Toyota remained totally independent of such 'technical co-operation' agreements. While the production of the Kaiser Henry J two-door didn't break any records, or rescue the Kaiser-Frazer company in the US, it did help Mitsubishi in other ways. Specifically, it gave the company a foot in the door when Kaiser-Frazer took over Willys, allowing Mitsubishi to build an off-road type vehicle in the early 1950s and then continue with its successors until the 1990s.

Mitsubishi steadily increased the range of cars and commercial vehicles it was producing. This included models like the three-wheeled Leo, and the two-door 500 saloon, which became the Colt 600 when the twin-cylinder engine was bored out to 594cc. One of Mitsubishi's most durable model ranges began in 1961 when the Minica – a four-wheel development of the Leo – arrived. The Minica is still around today, although it is now in its ninth series.

Mitsubishi moved from strength to strength over the next decade, introducing more models and producing a rapidly expanding number of cars. The next company landmark would be passed in 1969, when the Mitsubishi Motors Corporation was formed. This was still joined to the parent company of Mitsubishi Heavy Industries, but the vehicle production levels were such that MMC could definitely stand on its own.

Within a couple of years the Colt Galant was finding buyers in the USA through the Chrysler network. This company had initially held a 15 per cent share of MMC, but had upped this to 35 per cent by the middle of 1971.

Then, in 1973, came the launch of a new model, which happened to be the first-generation Lancer. Although the name has been around for 30 years now, the competitive streak was established early when a team of four Lancer 1600GSRs was sent to compete in the Australian Southern Cross Rally. Not only did all four cars finish on their maiden competitive outing, but they astounded everyone by taking the first four places.

Above: For many, the Evo V represents the ultimate Evolution. This was the first of the big-arched, big-winged, sharp-edged monsters, and it has a raw edge missing from the later, Cedia-based Evo VII and VIII. (Paul Buckland)

Next page: Here's a photographic representation of Darwin's Theory of Evolution, made metal. A dominant force in World Rallying until the Evo VII, let's hope the earlier success can be recaptured by the Evo VIII in 2004. (Ralliart Europe)

Evolution of the Mitsubishi Lancer Evo

Further Information From: Press Office, Tel: 01285 647200, e-mail: pressoffice@mitsubishi-cars.co.uk, FEB 2003, MM 1158

1992 - Evo I

1993 - Evo II

1995 - Evo III

1996 - Evo IV

1998 - Evo V

1999 - Evo VI

2001 - Evo VII

2003 - Evo VIII

Chapter **One**

In the beginning...

Tracing a vehicle model's history is generally an easy thing to do: you just go back through the manufacturer's catalogues looking at other incarnations of cars that bear the same name. When you get to the oldest example, you're done. But in the Mitsubishi Lancer Evolution's case it's not quite so simple.

It's not that the early vehicles are shrouded in mystery – although, because they were never UK models for the majority of their lives, information from and interest in official circles is almost non-existent. It's just that the Evo draws parts and systems from other non-Lancer models in the Mitsubishi line-up, and some of its competition forebears were almost one-off

specials in their own right. This means that to trace the lineage of the Lancer properly, we have to cover some ground that arguably belongs in the chapter dealing with competition history. However, it fits in better here and gives a clearer picture of where Evos really come from.

If we go back to the first-generation Lancer's competition debut in 1973, we soon find out that

The earliest Lancers were a far cry from the Evolution supercars that would follow in the 1990s, but when Joginder Singh took this 1974 GSR non-turbo Lancer to victory on the Safari Rally he proved how tough and resilient they were going to be.

The first Lancer Turbo was a Group 4 machine, and it showed promise during the 1982 season. A change to Group A/B/N regulations for the following year saw Mitsubishi leave the World Rally Championship until they could develop a successor.

motorsport was seen by Mitsubishi as a great way to improve its cars. In particular, international and world rally championships were chosen because of the fierce competition which exists at the top level of these gruelling formats. Success came in the most inhospitable conditions and gave the Lancer a start that showed real promise.

Although Mitsubishi competed quite successfully in those early years, the first car to bear the Lancer name that we should really be interested in arrived on the rough stuff when two cars entered the Acropolis Rally in June 1981. Sadly, the Group 4-homologated, works 280bhp turbocharged Lancer EX2000s didn't have a very auspicious debut. Both cars retired early in the event due to unrelated mechanical problems. But you have to be made of stern stuff to compete in any form of motorsport, and rallying at World Championship level is particularly tough. So the team moved to Finland for the

1000 Lakes event and, to add to their stress levels, they fielded an extra car too. Although the vehicles had some minor problems during this competition all three were helped by the cooler temperatures and finished the rally. The highest-placed car managed to come home in tenth position. By the end of the year the best result achieved by a Lancer EX2000 came in the RAC Rally, when one of them finished ninth.

The 1982 season was most notable for a major shake-up of rallying's homologation regs, and the Group 1 to Group 4 classes changed to Groups A, B, and N. Even though a small team like Mitsubishi wasn't in a position to move as quickly as some other organisations and get on the pace immediately, it did have a podium place – third – on the 1000 Lakes event that year. However, that was the only notable trophy gained during the season and, because it couldn't get cars ready in time for the new regs for 1983, the team withdrew from competition to regroup.

It wasn't until halfway through 1984 that Mitsubishi made a reappearance on the rally scene, in the shape of a four-wheel-drive Starion. This had a great debut at the French Mille Pistes rally, where it won the Prototype

class, but little real success followed at the top level of the sport. By 1986 it had been redeveloped as a two-wheel-drive vehicle and again had some success at lower levels of competition. But a big break eluded it as every other manufacturer's rally development moved on at high speed.

The next vehicle to be given the rough-stuff treatment by Mitsubishi was the Galant VR-4. It first competed in June 1988 at the Olympus Rally in America, where things went quite well and the Group N car finished in tenth place overall. From there the development of the Group A car saw some good results achieved through the rest of the 1988 season. The first wins were taken

DID YOU KNOW?

If you think Lancers were thrown in at the deep end when it came to rallying, spare a thought for the Mitsubishi Pajero, or Shogun as it was known in the UK. Introduced in 1983, the car was almost immediately put into the gruelling Paris–Dakar event, where it won its class. The following year the Pajero won its class again, and it's been well up there ever since.

The four-wheel-drive Starion Turbo first saw service on the 1984 Milles Pistes, where it took the Prototype category with Lasse Lampi behind the wheel.

the following year in the 1000 Lakes and the British RAC events.

By this time the Galant's specification made impressive reading. The turbocharged 2.0-litre motor produced a solid 290bhp, and the four-wheel-drive and four-wheel-steer car had a chassis that could successfully use its power on the sort of terrain that you'd struggle to walk over, never mind drive. Having found a platform that seemed to work well under rally conditions, the Mitsubishi engineers worked on developing the Galant's abilities. By the end of the 1990 season it was also equipped with a viscous-coupled centre differential that employed a 50:50 torque split.

The following season's changes included bigger brakes, made possible by an increase in wheel and tyre sizes, and then on the Greek Acropolis Rally the Galant VR-4 Evolution appeared on the scene. This car boasted more power to test its more competent chassis,

Above: Andrew Cowan drove many Mitsubishis before he took on the challenge of running Ralliart Europe. Here he is on the 1985 Paris–Dakar rally in a Pajero/Shogun.

Below: Although this is a Galant instead of a Lancer, the Evo's engine and transmission began life in this model, being refined and improved before the fourth-gen Lancer arrived to take on the WRC.

Kenneth Eriksson shows the Galant VR-4 was just as at home in the snow on the 1991 Swedish rally.

producing over 300bhp from its four-cylinder, 16-valve motor. Easy to spot as the 'cooking' version, the Galant VR-4 Evolution had gained a bigger intercooler as well as a louvered bulge on the bonnet. Although it showed plenty of ability, it didn't actually win an event until the Ivory Coast in 1990.

This event fell to Mitsubishi again the following year, but there was very little else to celebrate during that season. The programme of continuous development meant that the viscous-coupled diff was now electronically controlled, and that the torque split had been amended to 30 per cent front, 70 per cent rear, to improve handling. But there was no getting around the fact that for this kind of competition, the Galant was just a bit too heavy and a bit too big.

For these reasons, the 1992 season was to be the Galant VR-4's last in competition. Mitsubishi knew it had to build a car that was quicker, lighter, and more easily threaded through the rigours of the varied terrain that rallying threw at it. What it needed was the new, fourth-generation Lancer, and Mitsubishi already had the bolt-on goodies they required to make it a winner.

One of the mainstays of the Lancer Evolution's performance was – and still is – its turbocharged 4G63 powerplant. This had first appeared in the Galant VR-4, where it was progressively tweaked to around 300bhp, although this output was reduced before it

was fitted to the first Lancer Evolution models in 1992.

Mitsubishi was one of the many motor manufacturers who went down the forced-induction route in the early 1970s but, unlike a lot of the competition, who couldn't make turbocharged motors work well or reliably enough, Mitsubishi has stuck with it throughout. And when other companies were off experimenting with developments like multiple cams and valve arrangements on normally-aspirated engines, Mitsubishi did it in conjunction with its trusty turbochargers.

The other mainstay of the Evolution is the four-wheel-drive system that came from the Galant VR-4, although the transmission has been developed far beyond what was used at the turn of the 1990s. Now it's an incredibly sophisticated drivetrain that can put to work the boisterous power output afforded by the 4G63 motor in almost any conditions, safely and predictably.

So, having reviewed some of the earlier lineage of what was eventually to become one of the most successful rally cars of recent years, and a stunning road car available at an incredibly low price, let's move on to examine the first Lancer to bear the Evolution name.

Chapter Two

Evolution I, II, and III: the legend begins

Evolution – *ev-a-loo-shan, n* gradual working out or development, a series of things following in sequence.

Evolution I

The fourth-generation Mitsubishi Lancer was launched during October 1991, but, looking through the initial model range, there was nothing to tell anyone that a future competition legend was about to be unveiled.

There were several four-wheel-drive variants in the new Lancer line-up, and two of them were even powered by turbocharged 1.8-litre engines that gave respectable performance. But the new star only rose when the Lancer Evolution was announced in September 1992.

Once the Evolution was released for sale the following month, its immediate popularity took Mitsubishi by surprise. In order to satisfy the Fédération

Below: The chunky intercooler visible through the lower bumper opening hinted at the turbocharged lump hidden beneath the bonnet. The car might have looked pretty unassuming but its 250bhp clout made it a formidable road car.

Opposite: While not as radical-looking as some of the rally replicas around in 1992, the Evo I was adorned with scoops, grilles and spoilers. And none of them was cosmetic, they all had a real purpose.

Interesting snail's-eye view of the Evo I shows the relatively small 15in rims and lack of lower-body aerodynamic aids. Back in 1992 this was cutting edge technology, but in the next ten years the car would really live up to its name.

Internationale de l'Automobile (FIA) Group A regulations, a minimum of 2,500 cars needed to be produced. And, because changes to the body styling and aerodynamic add-ons weren't allowed, and engine and mechanical components were strictly controlled, the basic machine had to be right on the pace or the full-blown rally version would always be lagging behind its competition. However, the team behind the car weren't sure just how many of the stripped-down, raucous, motorsport-biased RS Lancers they could shift, so they introduced the slightly more plush GSR version at the same time to widen the appeal and help to boost sales.

The Powers That Be at Mitsubishi needn't have worried. When they had hoped rallying would increase the Lancer's popularity they had been absolutely right. All 2,500 cars sold out within three days, and instead of being left with cars cluttering up their overstock car parks, production of another 2,500 was sanctioned to keep the clamouring punters happy. It was easy to see why. A 250bhp, four-wheel-drive saloon that could race, commute, or carry four or five people in comfort was quite a mix, and it's one that still works today. Soon

DID YOU KNOW?

While everyone was blown away by the wild look of both homologation Ford Cosworths, the little Lancer Evolution had roughly 25bhp more power than the best Escort and was almost 50bhp ahead of the regular three-door Sierra.

everyone was raving about the LanEvo, as Japanese fans christened it.

The first Lancer Evolution was based on the GSR 1.8 Turbo. This model was chosen for a couple of reasons, mainly the stiffness of the four-door shell and the comparatively long wheelbase contained within its compact overall dimensions. Another factor was that the Lancer's rear suspension layout was much more simple than the complicated multi-link version fitted to the new model Galant VR-4.

It had been noted during discussions with motorsport engineers that the rally service crews would have something of a nightmare trying to fix a Galant's rear corner if one was 'modified' by a heavy impact during a stage. Simply put, the fourth generation Lancer was just the right size and level of complexity to base a real rally contender on. But there wasn't much of the basic car left under the skin once it had been modded for the job.

The suspension was fairly close to the original car's, though, with MacPherson struts at the front and Mitsubishi's well-regarded multi-link set-up at the rear. For the Evo it was uprated, with anti-roll bars front and rear and pillow-ball mounts at the rear end instead of rubber bushes on the upper and lower arms, and outer control links. Because the Lancer Evo was a road car in spite of all its homologation leanings, the spring and damper rates were left soft enough to be lived with on a daily basis.

The Evo's wheel and tyre combination had to take into account that the Lancer body struggled to accommodate huge rims and rubber. With this in mind, the standard GSR wheels were 15in alloy, wrapped in 195/55VR15 tyres. Hidden under the rims were ventilated discs and two-pot sliding calipers at the front end, and solid discs with single-pot sliding calipers at the rear. Four-wheel ABS was a standard fitment.

The body of the Evo was also the subject of some hefty tweaks to make it suitable as a rally platform. Although the original car was reasonably light and strong, the Evo shell was strengthened in several key areas around the front end so that it could cope with the increased mass of the heavier engine/ transmission unit, and the bigger loads that would come from the power hike and off-road action. The strengthening mods resulted in an increase in

The first use of the 4G63 two-litre engine in the Lancer shows how neatly it fitted into the small engine bay, even with all its ancillary goodies. It would be a few years until the engine was swapped round and given its famous red cam cover, but everything has to start somewhere.

The Evo I's simple rear spoiler did have beneficial aerodynamic qualities without dominating the car's back end. But as rallying became faster, so the spoilers would grow.

Just in case you'd forgotten what you were looking at, Mitsubishi put on a few helpful reminders.

torsional rigidity of around 20 per cent, but at the expense of some added weight. To offset this unwanted penalty the car's panel vibration damping material was omitted.

The front-to-rear balance was also improved when an aluminium bonnet was employed to save weight at the front end. The nose was dominated by the large intercooler aperture in the Evo-exclusive one-piece grille/bumper moulding and the lamp mounts alongside it. The lower grille had to be moved well forward to fit over the chunky front-mounted intercooler. Above the businesslike nose the bonnet was also swiss-cheesed with a small air intake on the driver's side, and a couple of larger louvered vents cut into the centre for releasing heated air from the engine bay.

The Evo-only body mods continued at the rear end with a large boot-mounted spoiler that was designed to reduce lift at high speed. Although it was considered huge at the time, it wasn't quite as outrageous as the one fitted to, say, the Sierra three-door or Escort Cosworth, but it did the job by lowering lift some 18 per cent.

Hidden away under the bonnet was a version of the engine that had done such sterling service powering the Galant VR-4. This had been given a few tweaks in preparation for its new job. The top end sported new fuel injectors, a reworked cylinder head that contained new sodium-filled valves, and a raised compression ratio – up to 8.5:1 from the Galant's 7.8:1. The bottom end was all new, with a lightweight

Left: Standard Mitsubishi alloy wheels are a bit rare on early Evos now. Because of the Lancer's tight wheel-arch clearance there wasn't room for anything much bigger, but that would be worked on over the next few models.

Although most of the cabin furnishings were straight out of the Lancer parts bins, the Evo did get a leather-wrapped Momo steering wheel to improve the driver-to-car interface.

The supportive Recaro seats were a standard fitment, giving a comfortable and multi-adjustable driving position for all sizes of Evo pilot.

crankshaft and new connecting rods and pistons. Work had also been done on reducing the motor's internal friction in order to help throttle response, particularly at higher engine speeds. Keeping the 85 x 88mm bore and stroke gave a 1,997cc capacity, and the power output was quoted as 250PS (246bhp) at 6,000rpm, with a torque figure of 308.8Nm (228lb/ft) at 3,000rpm. This was only a 10PS increase over the VR-4 lump but that 250PS was dragging round quite a bitless weight.

The turbocharger used on this version of the 4G63 engine was a TD05H-16G-7 unit. It was connected to a bigger intercooler that wouldn't strangle the motor's appetite for cool intake air. The intercooler also had a small water spray jet aimed at it so that the driver could squirt cool fluid onto the radiator core if the intake temperature was getting too high. The water came from the windscreen washer bottle, so it looked like the design team were either hoping that you wouldn't need

to squirt the intercooler when it was raining, or that you wouldn't need to wash the screen when you were driving hard. At the other side of the turbo was a large-bore exhaust system which lowered restrictive back pressure. The system ended in twin pipes that exited to the left-hand end of the rear bumper.

Transmitting this healthy power output through to the five-speed gearbox was an uprated clutch unit, and the synchro on second gear was also swapped for a double-cone type. This mod was done to reduce the shift effort and increase the durability of second gear. The gearbox itself was a close-ratio design so the driver could be sure of having a cog available to keep the motor on the boil, and the same 'box was used on both GSR and RS variants.

The four-wheel-drive system was the same as had been developed on the Galant over the last couple of rally seasons, and boasted viscous-coupled centre and LSD rear differentials. It probably goes without saying

that an automatic gearbox wasn't made available, but I thought I'd mention it anyway.

Even if there wasn't a slushbox to calm down the driver and help him to relax a bit, Mitsubishi didn't expect Evo pilots to suffer too much for their art, especially if you bought the GSR version. Creature comforts included air conditioning, bronze-tinted glass in the electric windows, a leather-trimmed Momo wheel to twirl the power steering, a tilt-adjustable column, and a matching gearknob.

Super-supportive Recaro seats took care of driver and front passenger location, there was a driver's foot rest, electric remote-control door mirrors, six-speaker stereo, and more. Perhaps one of the more unusual standard features was the rear screen wash/wipe, although these have always seemed a great idea to me, even on a saloon car.

To save weight – bearing in mind how Mitsubishi saw this version being used – the RS lost some of the added fripperies unnecessary for competition. Off came the ABS, air conditioning, the majority of the electrical doodads, the rear wash/wipe, and some interior trim bits. The comfy Recaros were also swapped for more basic seats, the rear LSD was swapped for a mechanical one, and the alloy wheels were changed for steelies. In exchange for losing all these nice touches the RS driver would end up with a car that was 70kg (154lb) lighter than the GSR. Mitsubishi reckoned that most RSs would end up in competition so there was no point in fitting good seats or posh wheels when a competitor would change them for real race-spec equipment.

Another area where the RS owner lost out was colour choice. While the GSR was available in white, silver, red, green, and black, the RS customer had to choose between white and silver. Still, when you're only going to cover it in loads of stickers and race numbers, who cares?

The result of all this Evolutionary fettling was a car that weighed over 200kg (441lb) less than the Galant

Even if it was the basis of a rally car, the Evo GSR still had extras like sophisticated air conditioning and a reasonable six-speaker radio-cassette audio system. It was the RS that was the no-frills version.

VR-4 (Galant 1,350kg/2,977lb, Evo GSR 1,240kg/2,734lb, Evo RS 1,170kg/2,580lb), had more power, and was much more nimble. And Mitsubishi didn't think it would sell? What were they on?

To find out how the Evolution I performed in the heat of competition, have a look at the rally history chapter further on; but for now, let's move on to the Evo II and see what Mitsubishi did to improve on one of the strongest opening models they ever released.

Evolution II

Despite having sold out ridiculously quickly, the Lancer Evolution I technically remained on Mitsubishi's books until they announced the replacement Evo II in December 1993. Based on how well the buying public had taken to the previous model, the new version was slated for a 5,000-car production run from the beginning. It was another hit, selling out in just three months.

Mitsubishi had started the Lancer Evolution project with an overall plan to increase the engine output by

Outwardly very similar to the Evo I, the Evo II had a new lower lip spoiler on the front end. Other change were equally subtle, but still worthwhile.

DID YOU KNOW?

Although the Evo II weighed 10kg (22lb) more than the Evo I, the body's torsional rigidity, so Mitsubishi claimed, had gone up 30 per cent. That's a 0.8 per cent increase in body weight, so it's not much of a penalty really, is it?

10PS with each new model until they reached the Japanese domestic power limit of 280PS (276bhp). This would be accompanied by an appropriate increase in brakes and suspension to cope with the extra power as needed. They also wanted to improve any deficiencies that showed up when the cars were actually being used in the real world. When they came to work on Evo II they had a few ideas on what needed to be tweaked.

The main areas to be improved were noted as handling, traction, and stability, with the previous model suffering from a little too much understeer. The tarmac-handling performance also had to be addressed because of the increase in the number of tarmac stages on the new World Rally calendar. To sort out these areas Mitsubishi's engineers went through the suspension system and revised almost every

Above: The Evo II's rear spoiler grew slightly in stature with the addition of the lower section, known as the wicker. This car has also had some rally-style mud flaps and a non-standard exhaust fitted.

Left: The new model's badging was quite restrained. Enthusiasts would be able to tell the new model from its predecessor just by looking, but anyone else would have to check carefully to find out what they were looking at.

Opposite: This Evo II has been given a performance air filter, a new recirculating dump valve and a strut brace to help improve both its performance and poise.

Above left: It might not say 'turbo', 'fuel injection' or 'twin cam' but those in the know gave it the respect it deserved.

Above right: This detail close-up shows the moulded Evolution II script in the wicker, and the high-level brake light built into the spoiler blade. This was so you could see that the Evo in front of you had been braking a lot less than you were while it was pulling away...

Left: From the other side of the spoiler you can see that the wicker isn't just a simple wedge, it has an aerodynamic profile that improves downforce without incurring too much extra drag.

dimension. While the overall length and width of the car was unchanged, the wheelbase was increased, as was the front and rear track.

These parameters weren't altered by much. The front track was widened by 15mm (0.58in) and the rear by 10mm (0.39in), and the front wheel arches were reworked inside to accommodate larger wheels and tyres. The wheelbase went up by 10mm by dint of moving the front wheels forward, which also called for wheel arch mods. Once there was more room under the front wings, Mitsubishi were safe to use 205/60/HR15 tyres. As before, these were fitted to either alloy wheels on the GSR – this time supplied by OZ Racing – or steel rims on the RS.

While the chassis dimensions were being amended, the suspension geometry was tweaked and the mounting points were strengthened too. The front anti-roll bar was decreased in section from 23mm to 16mm (0.90in to 0.62in) and the lower suspension arm was changed for a forged item which was much stronger. The front struts were changed and the damper stroke was lengthened, while the camber angle was also realigned.

The final touch was an amended steering rack that required less turns from lock to lock and a new power steering pump. At the rear end the only work to be done was increasing the spring rate. The result of these small amendments was that the Evo II's handling and steering was much improved, and that the car was 25mm (1in) taller than the Evo I.

To keep to the plan of increasing engine power with each Evolution model, Mitsubishi raised the boost pressure acting on the motor and fitted a freer-flowing exhaust system. These mods worked together with increased valve lift and netted the required 10PS gain, although the torque figure remained the same.

Because of the new 260PS (256bhp) output the clutch and gearbox came in for a little attention too, a beefier clutch plate being used and double-cone synchros being fitted to third and fourth gears. The rear LSD was also changed so that both the GSR and RS versions had a mechanical unit.

From an exterior viewpoint the Evo II didn't look a lot different to its predecessor, but those in the know could spot the changes immediately. The front bumper had

grown a small double chin in the form of a lower airdam and the rear spoiler was fitted with a new lower section called a wicker. This was also embossed with an Evolution II script, just in case anyone hadn't figured out what kind of car they were looking at.

Inside the cockpit there were a few detail changes, beginning with new Recaro seats that were even more supportive and better at locating an occupant than the earlier ones. Apart from that there was an improvement in some electrical items, and the air conditioning system went over to CFC-free refrigerant gas. The Momo steering wheel was the same design that had been used in the Evo I, but this time it was used in both the GSR and RS. The RS was also offered with a vinyl-trimmed interior to reinforce the no-nonsense motorsport connection. Final amendments to the Evo II concerned the colours, with a blue taking over from the green that had been offered on the GSR, and the RS now only being available in white.

The results of all these small alterations were exactly as anticipated. The Evo was quicker, and its traction and steering were much improved, so it could use more of the power more of the time. The cost of all this work was a small 10kg (22lb) hike in the weight of both the GSR and RS models, more than compensated for by the 10PS gain. Although it looked very similar to its predecessor, the Evo II was a real step forward and showed the way for future Evos – onward and upward.

Evolution III

Fans of the Lancer Evolution only had to wait until January 1995 for the next stage in the car's development to be announced. The Evo III went on sale in February, with 5,000 available for the public to snap up.

Power output had been increased by the expected 10PS again, this time by little more work than a boost tweak and a new pipe as on the Evo II. New pistons were used to raise the compression ratio from 8.5:1 to 9.0:1 and the engine tuning was amended to run stronger at higher revs. The new power figure of 270PS (266bhp) was made at 6,250rpm, but the torque output remained the same as the two previous cars.

A new TD05-16G6-7 turbocharger fitted with a larger compressor was now employed and the exhaust system was changed to one that was less restrictive by using a fatter front pipe and a freer-flowing main silencer box. The single intercooler spray nozzle fitted to the earlier cars was doubled up, so that the incoming charge temperature could be lowered further and kept at a stable level when the motor was working hard for long

Opposite: Getting cool air through into a turbo engine's underbonnet area is hugely important for efficient running, hence the large intakes in the Evo's front end. And keeping the brakes cool is also a good idea when there's so much speed potential to play with.

When the Evo III arrived it had metamorphosised into something much more aggressive than the two previous versions. This is a rare RS version and, as Mitsubishi had planned, the supplied steel wheels have been replaced with after-market alloys.

Above: Telltale RS giveaways include the black door handles and mirrors. A manual aerial exiting from the top of the driver's door pillar is another clue that this is the basic version and destined for competitive off-road use.

Below: From this angle you can see the large side skirts, rear corner extensions and new rear spoiler that showed the aerodynamics crew had been burning the midnight oil in the wind tunnel.

The deep side skirts proved the ideal place to emboss the Evo III's new nomenclature.

The rear badging was a tad more discreet than earlier models, in complete contrast to the additional spoilers the car was wearing.

The Evo III had a proper wing element in the spoiler instead of just being a hoop. More downforce was required as rally stage speeds increased and the focus of competition moved more towards tarmac events.

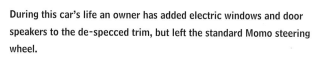

The RS trim levels were a little more rudimentary than the GSR's. Here you can see there's just s simple piece of carpet to cover the spare wheel and no other boot liners to add to the car's overall weight.

During this car's life an owner has added electric windows and door speakers to the de-specced trim, but left the standard Momo steering wheel.

periods. What that did to the length of time between washer bottle refills wasn't noted.

Even though there was marginally more power to deal with the gearbox and clutch were unchanged, but the final-drive ratio was made a little higher. Again both the GSR and RS used the same close-ratio gearbox. The same wheel and tyre options were also offered on the Evo III.

The big changes came in the aero package, which came about because of the way rallying was changing. More tarmac stages meant higher speeds, so properly controlling the air flowing over, under, and through the Lancer was becoming more and more important with each event. The most noticeable addition on the front end was the new bumper moulding and lower spoiler that came complete with ducts to direct cooling air towards each front brake assembly, as well as to the centre-mounted transmission transfer case. By extending the spoiler towards the ground, the amount of air slipping underneath the body was reduced, improving the car's drag and reducing the amount of lift induced at high speeds.

The front bumper became a lot more aggressive than on the previous cars, with the side intakes in particular growing into real widemouth scoops. The lower profile of the front spoiler was carried along the sides of the car with new skirts that also bore the all-important Evolution III badging. This style line was continued onto the rear bumper with lower corner splitters, which had a beneficial effect on the way the car left the air behind it. And, even though the Evo III's appearance was markedly different to the Evo II, the overall dimensions were exactly the same.

Wind tunnel work also threw up a new design of rear spoiler with an even bigger wicker than before, and a real wing element rather than the hoop-style spoilers used previously. This spoiler combination produced more downforce than before, but with little drag penalty, which was just as important. The only slight downside was that the new placement of the high-level brake light in the rear edge of the wicker meant there was nowhere for the model badging that had graced the Evo II. Still, there was some room for a smaller badge on the boot lid itself, and with the large lettering in the side skirts and the much more aggressive look all round it wasn't a car that hid its identity. Also new for the Evo III was a vivid yellow colour that replaced the blue used on the last version. The RS was again only made available in white.

As for interior changes, the Evo III had to make do

with a new fabric covering for the same style Recaro seats, while the old Momo steering wheel design was swapped for a much more up-to-date model known as the 'Speed Three'. The RS fell out of step by keeping the same type of Momo it had been using through the Evo II's lifespan.

In a similar vein to the Evo II changes, the new additions to the Evo III cost it an additional 10kg (22lb), but the benefits of the better aerodynamics were worth more than that alone. You can see just what impact the changes had on the Evo III's competitive history a little later, but if you're staying for the history lesson, turn the page and find out what Mitsubishi had been brewing to replace the first generation of Evolutions.

These Cobra seats were fitted to replace the standard perches that were decidedly low-rent. Having larger side bolsters they will hold the occupants in position much better during the sort of cornering the Evo's abilities encourage.

Chapter **Three**

Lancer Evolution IV, V, and VI: bigger, better, faster, more!

Evolution IV

When Mitsubishi rolled out the fifth-generation Lancer in October 1995, it was an obvious improvement over the previous model. Cosmetically it was a sharper looking design, but underneath the nicely-cut suit was a body that had been designed with computer technology. This allowed more strength to be added without any additional weight penalty.

From every angle it looked like a more modern car and, although the dimensions were within millimetres of the old model, there was more interior and luggage space. Not only was it more occupant-friendly because of the work Mitsubishi had done on refining the ergonomics and noise, vibration, and harshness levels, it also passed international safety standards with ease. The icing on the cake, as far as the manufacturer was concerned, was that it was less costly to make, so prices could be amended without cutting the profits needed for further development work.

While the new model was being launched around the world, Mitsubishi's Lancer Evolution III was still racking up the points in the World Rally Championship. So at the end of 1995 and during the early months of 1996 there was a slightly odd situation where the previous model was still being rallied while the new one was being sold.

For the first time in Mitsubishi's production history, a new mainstream model had been designed with a motorsport variant from the outset. This meant that the fifth-gen Lancer had its engine rotated 180° to the fourth-gen design, and a new four-wheel-drive transmission system was used

that would have benefits when it came to the rally version.

Eager motorsport fans had to wait until the end of July 1996 before the Evolution IV was officially announced, and it became available in August. It seems Mitsubishi were cautiously optimistic about sales of the new car, because it produced 6,000 of them, 20 per cent more than it had done in the past. It was wrong about the production number, though, and after the first cars had sold out in three days it had to produce another 3,000 to satisfy its overflowing order books.

Although the body was all new, the basic recipe was the same. However, the Mitsubishi engineers hadn't just been planning another set of subtle upgrades for the new car – they had plenty of new ideas and new products to add to the already successful mix. But it was realised that the added complexity was going to cost them a fair amount of weight, so the first thing to do was balance the extra lard with extra beef. That meant the 4G63 motor was in for a major makeover. The famous red cam cover was also introduced at this time, distinguishing the new version of the 4G63 from its cousins in the earlier Evos. Hidden under the 'Mitsubishi' trim panel in this bigger cover was a pair of twin-plug coil packs that took over ignition duties from the system fitted to the previous cars.

The re-engineering job started with the fundamentals – the block and cylinder head. These were lightened by

Opposite: The Evolution IV was a totally new bodystyle, but all the lessons learnt on the previous versions were carried over. There was plenty of new stuff under the surface as well.

Above: The Evo IV was obviously something born for competition. More time spent analysing the way the air moved over and through the car resulted in the radical front end treatment. This had the added benefit of moving almost everything out of your way when on the public roads

Below: The rear spoiler had evolved back into a hoop, but the wicker had grown much larger than on earlier models. The new rear bumper also had extensions built-in to match the side skirts, rather than being tacked on as an afterthought.

Evolution badging looked more like the rest of the scripts used on the Evo IV, summing up that this version of Lancer was designed to have a tough rally derivative from the beginning.

Built-in driving lamps emphasised the competition character of the new car.

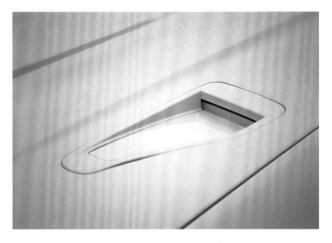

The NACA duct on the bonnet fed air approximately into the air filter area of the engine bay. And when performance is at stake, every little helps.

Even though it's a serious performance car the Evo IV has plenty of user-friendly features like this rear window wiper. When you've driven a non-hatchback with a rear wiper you'll wonder why all cars aren't fitted with them.

making them from thinner castings, and the rest of the motor was put on a diet to match. The pistons were now lightweight forged items which would stand up to the abuse of higher combustion pressures, even though the compression ratio had been dropped to 8.8:1. In a similar vein, a new steel head gasket was fitted to resist the planned boost pressure increase better.

Different camshafts were used with a profile that would work better at high revs, and a lightened flywheel was fitted to help the motor spin up faster. A new TD05HR-16G6-9T turbocharger was chosen to blow harder than before, and a larger intercooler was fitted so that it wouldn't hamper the extra gas flow.

To keep the turbo spooled up, a new exhaust manifold had been designed to minimise exhaust gas

interference, and a secondary air injection system helped to keep the turbo spinning during moments of deceleration. This improved the turbo response when the driver wanted to get back on the power because there wasn't that short delay, waiting for the turbo to start blowing again.

The new turbo was also a twin-scroll design, and it produced more boost lower down the rev range. This was coupled to a new design of intake manifold that had straighter tracts for improved gas flow, and these improvements netted a fatter torque curve through the low and mid-range rev band. A new exhaust design also helped the flow, and the twin tailpipes of the earlier cars were replaced by a single large-bore item.

The result of these extensive modifications was

another 10PS, meaning that the new Evo had continued the 10PS-increase target planned for each new version, and that it had now hit the Japanese power limit of 280PS (276bhp) at 6,500rpm. It doesn't sound like much of a gain for all those tweaks and clever new components, but 10PS isn't the full story. The torque output had risen sharply from the 308.8Nm (228lb/ft) at 3,000rpm of the Evo I–III to 352.9Nm (260lb/ft) at the same rev point.

This increase in usable mid-range power was there to compensate for all the added weight the rest of the car was carrying. The GSR version had bulked up by 90kg (198lb), while the RS model had put on 70kg

DID YOU KNOW?

For anyone who's easily befuddled by numbers, it's head-scratching time. When the fifth-generation Lancer was launched in October 1995, the Evo III – which was a first-gen Evo based on the fourth-gen Lancer – was still out there in competition. But the fifth-gen Lancer that was now on sale hadn't quite given birth to the Evo IV, which would be the first of the second-gen Evos. Confused?

The Evo IV was the model that saw the introduction of the red cam cover on the 4G63, and the reorientation of the motor in order to fit the new four-wheel-drive system. Under the new cover was a motor that produced more power and torque than ever before.

(154lb). This meant the weight difference between the two Evo IVs was widened to 90kg. It was a good job there was plenty of fresh new torque to shift it along, wasn't it?

To go with a vastly reworked engine there was an equally reworked transmission, and a new level of complexity had crept in to help keep the Evo on top of the rallying world. The most notable new feature was the Active Yaw Control (AYC) system which operated on the rear differential. This used a mix of computer control and hydraulic actuation that distributed the power split through the rear diff depending on cornering conditions. The correct technical explanation of what the AYC does reads: 'The system generates a stabilising yaw moment by creating a torque differential in the rear wheels' – which basically means that the electronics actuate the hydraulic system to alter the diff setting and divert more power to the outside wheel while the car is going through a bend. This helps to

The new Evo IV looked familiar from the driver's seat, but the Momo steering wheel now sported an airbag, and there was another fitted on the dash to give the passenger a broken nose and black eyes to match the driver . . .

keep the car on line, and improves its initial turn-in characteristics and its stability under heavy braking.

As well as AYC, the Evo IV GSR variant also had a viscous-coupled centre diff that provided a 50:50 torque split front to rear, and a helical-geared front diff. The transfer case was one of the items that had suffered due to the rotation of the engine, and because of this the case was bigger, heavier, and more expensive to make.

The RS wasn't burdened by the complex AYC system, relying on a mechanical LSD instead. It was felt that experienced drivers would prefer the car's abilities without the clever diff figuratively looking over their shoulder all the time, and that they could make better progress without it. But the lack of AYC was more than made up for because the front diff was a torque-adaptive helical-gear LSD, and this was the first time a four-wheel drive production car had been kitted out with such a device.

A new five-speed gearbox was also produced for Evo

IV use, having shorter throws between gear positions. The Evo IV was the first of the Mitsubishis to use a different set of ratios for GSR and RS versions, and the RS also had a choice of high or low final-drive ratios. These changes were made with motorsport in mind, so that a competitor could tune the transmission ratios to suit a particular event.

The new Evo's body design housed a revised multi-link rear suspension layout, and the geometry of the MacPherson strut front suspension was amended to suit the new forces acting on it. The bigger car now had room for slightly larger wheels under the new wheel arches, so a neat 12-spoke, 6.5J x 16in OZ alloy was chosen to support the Evo IV, and these rims were wrapped in 205/50/VR16 rubber.

Keeping to the tradition set by the earlier three models, the Evo IV RS was offered with 15in steel rims and HR-rated tyres from the factory. Because of the lack of room inside these wheels, it was fitted with the smaller brakes from the Evo III, but there were other options available. In fact, the RS could be purchased in five options that mixed and matched wheel size, brake size, AYC fitment or deletion, and gearbox and final-drive ratios. For a motorsport contestant it was a great

Opposite: Even though it had masses of power and was devastatingly quick, the Evo IV could take five adult people without being uncomfortable. Try that in a 911!

Right: The early Evos were Japanese market only, and had interesting features like electric folding door mirrors, presumably for getting into incredibly tight parking spaces. But, if the space is that narrow, how does the driver then get out?

idea to have such a varied menu to choose from, and it ensured that anyone buying the car for sporting use got a vehicle that was optimised for the type of events it would be entering.

Carrying the extra weight while still having better performance would put extra strain on the braking system, so an upgrade was fitted in the shape of larger ventilated discs all round. These were still gripped by twin- and single-piston sliding calipers, but the 294mm front and 284mm rear discs provided plenty of swept area to grab hold of. As you'd probably expect, ABS was still fitted as standard to keep the braking performance as safe and predictable as possible.

The new Lancer body style not only looked more modern than the one it replaced, it had been designed to slice through the air better too. In Evolution form it was still covered in the usual spoilers, wings, and vents, but their performance had been thoroughly tested and honed to get the most improvement possible. As a brief aside, the new car was 20mm (0.78in) longer, but 5mm (0.19in) lower and narrower, although the wheelbase was the same. The front track had been widened by 20mm so that front and rear track were identical at 1,470mm (57.33in).

The new integrated front bumper and grille moulding held a large pair of PIAA spot lamps on either side of the gaping maw that allowed air unhindered access onto the core of the intercooler. The side vent on the driver's side of the bumper also directed air through onto the engine oil cooler. Below the bumper was an additional spoiler to help keep as much air as possible from getting under the car and inducing unwanted lift.

Larger side skirts followed the styling cue from the front end's lower spoiler, and had a beneficial effect on the air flowing around the rear wheels too. And instead of the small lower corner trims fitted to the Evo III, the Evo IV had a full lower spoiler section that wrapped around the bottom edge of the back bumper and had a

cut-out to allow the slightly oval exhaust to sit a little further away from the ground.

Dominating the rear end was the revised two-piece spoiler that had grown to such large proportions that it almost completely covered the boot lid. The wicker had taken on such a large delta shape that it nearly touched the rear window. Whatever you thought of the look of the car – and most people loved its brutal presence – you couldn't argue that the aerodynamic additions were all for show, because they certainly worked. Not only had the Mitsubishi team reduced the coefficient of drag to Cd 0.30 – a figure that had been touted as just about the best possible when Audi launched the weird-looking 100 back in 1982 – they'd done it whilst completely eliminating aerodynamic lift, which was quite a feat.

As well as the body being very efficient for drag-free high speed use, it was also very strong. A combination of lots of additional spot welding and reinforcing pieces stiffened the basic shell at key points like the front strut towers, scuttle, and upper body, as well as across the opening behind the rear seats. To stiffen things even further the RS was fitted with a bolt-on upper strut bar that braced the strut towers against each other, and an additional front cross member.

To update the interior Mitsubishi called on the same people to supply them with the new bits. The front seats were Recaros again, but they were slightly different in shape to those of the Evo III, as was the trim material. The steering wheel was still a Momo design, but now it had an SRS airbag, and a matching airbag was fitted to the passenger-side dashboard. While these devices were standard offerings on the GSR, the pared-down RS lacked such safety items because it didn't need any more weight to carry round. It also used a different Momo wheel. The final touch was a white dial set carried in a new dashboard.

Although most of the equipment spec was carried over from the Evo III, there were a few changes.

The tinted glass was now green, and the well-specced stereo system was dropped onto the option list, where it was joined by heated door mirrors and, from the month after it was launched, a Ralliart Sports Pack.

For some reason the colour choice for the GSR had meanwhile become a little more conservative, dropping the bright yellow and reinstating a pearl mid-blue to go with white, silver, black, and red. And no prizes for guessing which single colour the RS was sold in...

Bearing in mind the Evo IV was a more-or-less totally new model rather than a simple mid-term revamp, it performed brilliantly out of the box. And even though it was quite a bit heavier than its forerunners, it wasn't seen as an overweight boxer who'd gone to seed and should stop before he got hurt. Instead, the Evo IV was a fighter that had just gone up a weight and now had more energy behind that deadly punch. Sales figures showed how popular the IV was and rally results proved the design was a real winner. It was getting to the stage where everyone expected each new version of the four-door supercar to be a step up the Evolutionary ladder, and they waited impatiently to see what Mitsubishi would come up with next.

Evolution V

If anyone had expected the Evolution V to be a similar small step forward from the IV, in the same way that the first three versions had progressed, they were in for a big shock. Well, more like a pleasant surprise really, because the Evo V was a great leap forward. Just looking at a IV and a V side by side showed how much had been altered cosmetically. And a quick scan of the new model's spec sheet would show how much work had gone on during the 18 months before the Evo V's release in January 1998.

The new body mods had been made with the World Rally Championship's Group A regulations in mind.

DID YOU KNOW?

Not only are Japanese cars power limited to 280PS (276bhp), they are speed limited to 180kph (112mph). That's why there are no official top speed figures for the Japanese-only Evolution models. Of course, when an Evo arrives in this country, a quick change to a UK speedo means the car is limited to 180mph (290kph).

Although a new category of World Rally Car had been announced at the beginning of 1997, Mitsubishi stuck to their guns and continued developing the Group A-based Evos rather than making a new competition-only vehicle as some of their rivals had done. This meant that anything Mitsubishi were rallying could be seen as a direct relative of something you could conceivably drive on the road. This was preferable to the one-off WRC chariots that would cost insane amounts of money and have no real relevance to the road cars they were supposedly based on.

To maximise the handling abilities of the latest Evo the front and rear tracks were widened quite dramatically. There was an extra 40mm (1.56in) in the front dimension and 35mm (1.37in) in the rear. These increases in girth were accompanied by a widening of the bodywork to the Group A maximum of 1,770mm (69in) to cover the larger wheel and tyre combination. The front wings were made from aluminium like the bonnet, and heavily flared to provide the tyre cover. The rear wheels were covered by additional blisters added to the rear door and wing.

Further aerodynamic improvements came about through the use of new front and rear bumpers and modified side skirts and rear apron. The front airdam was a new design, and the rear spoiler had become even more outrageous than before. Not only were the side supports more angular, allowing a larger spoiler blade to be fitted between them, but the blade was also four-position adjustable for attack angle.

Although these modifications were only updates of the equipment fitted to the Evo IV, the V looked much meaner than its predecessor. And, although the car was so much more angular and bigger in frontal area, the drag figure had only gone up to Cd 0.31, which was quite an achievement.

The bonnet came in for a large revision in the form of a new vent, which was considerably bigger than that used on the Evo IV. More cooling air was allowed into the engine bay by a larger front grille, and a bigger radiator was fitted in an effort to improve cooling efficiency. The engine oil cooler was also uprated to the same ends.

Because the motor had hit the Japanese manufacturers' self-imposed 280PS (276bhp) limit in the Evo IV, there was no increase in horsepower on the

Opposite: Looking like an Evo IV on steroids, the Evo V is an amazing looking car at rest or at speed. The body bulges in so many new areas it's often difficult to see the resemblance to the Evo IV.

Above: Those new aluminium wings cover the widest allowable track under Group A rally regulations, and make fitting large wheels and tyres easy.

Below: The rear quarters sprouted arch extensions to match the front end, and the new rear spoiler not only had a larger blade, it was adjustable for angle of attack to increase downforce when required.

Previous page: Getting cooling air into an engine bay is only half the job. It's just as important to get it out and away from the car as smoothly as possible. Hence this monster vent that has spawned numerous copies on other, less worthy cars.

Below: This is probably the most recognisable bit carried over from the Evo IV. Almost every other part of the Evo V's body had undergone some modification in the name of aerodynamic efficiency.

Below: This shot shows the four-way adjustability of the rear spoiler blade, and in this case it's set to its most neutral position. Although it will produce a lot less downforce in this setting, the benefits on fuel consumption and top speed through less drag will be easily noticed.

Bottom: That wicker is getting huge! No wonder there's room for the high-level brake light in it – you couldn't see it if it was fitted in the rear window.

Evo V, but the torque figure wasn't hampered by such an imposed maximum. The new figure of 372.6Nm (275lb/ft) was 19.6Nm (14.5lb/ft) up on the IV, and showed that the engine technicians had been just as busy as the aerodynamicists.

To achieve this small torque increase quite a list of modifications had been made to the 4G63. Another new turbocharger design with larger nozzle – a TD05HR-

Right: Wearing all the right labels, the Evo V showed off its Brembo brakes behind OZ Racing alloy wheels. The bigger brakes tried to keep pace with the ever-improving performance, while the lighter wheels helped the suspension provide better control and grip.

Below: This immaculate Evo V is just as clean under the lid as it is on the outside. And although it's standard at the moment, it probably won't be long before there are some tasteful modifications to give even better performance. There isn't even a strut brace.

16G6-10.5T this time – was used to improve engine response, particularly at higher revs. This was matched to a new intercooler and different lightweight pistons. With the increased capacities of the radiator and oil cooler, the engine could develop more grunt whilst remaining ultra reliable.

Moving to the transmission mods, the ratios remained the same as before, but the synchro mechanism and gearshift linkage were beefed up to improve durability and shift quality. Having made such a positive impact, the clever AYC system was continued in the Evo V. The RS model also retained all its possible ratio and final drive options to keep the competition driver happy.

While Mitsubishi stayed true to Recaro as their preferred seat supplier, Recaro worked with the Japanese company to improve the seats and make them ever lighter in line with the Evolutionary ethos.

Look familiar? An Evo IV pilot would be at home in an Evo V right away. Of course the difference in performance and handling might be a bit of a giveaway.

Filling those widened wheel arches was a set of 17in OZ alloys that looked very similar in pattern to the 16s that were used on the IV, but these were 7.5in (190mm) wide and wore 225/45/17 rubber. They were mounted on heavily revised suspension that had been changed to maximise grip and handling in line with the extra room afforded by the increased track measurements of the Group A maximum.

The front suspension had been fitted with a longer and stronger forged aluminium lower arm, and the front struts had been swapped for an inverted design that also

had a longer stroke. A new camber adjuster allowed fine tuning of steering characteristics, and the steering rack was moved slightly to further optimise handling. A new design of power steering pump meant that Mitsubishi's engineers could consign the old power steering oil cooler to the bin, saving a few valuable kilos. The rear suspension mounting points were altered to increase the track width, and the rear geometry was tweaked to lower the roll centre and to give better road-holding and improve cornering response. Like every Evo before it, the V just kept getting better.

Another benefit of fitting the bigger wheels was the adoption of some really serious brakes. The Evo finally had enough 'stop' to match its ever-increasing 'go'. The front brakes were 320mm vented discs gripped by very impressive four-pot Brembo calipers, while the rear set-up was swapped for 300mm discs fitted with twin-piston calipers. GSR models kept their ABS system too.

Although they were looking decidedly past their sell-by date, the wheels fitted to the RS models were still the 15in steelies. This had the old knock-on effect of holding the braking system at Evo III levels, but with the Evo V RS weighing in at 1,260kg (2,778lb) – the same as the Evo III GSR – they were still up to the job and would probably be swapped when the car went into battle anyway. In case you were wondering, the GSR had tried hard to diet, but ended up putting on 10kg (22lb) instead of shedding any. I know people who've been on diets like that.

The inside of the Evo V GSR was the area which remained closest to the IV, with only minor changes to the Recaro seat design and thinner glass to save a little weight. Apart from that there were the same dash and instruments with their white faces, and the twin airbags. RS models still had the poor-relation trim that did without the supportive Recaros or airbagged Momo steering wheel. The welcome return of a vivid yellow Evo meant that the pearl blue had been dropped again, while the white, black, silver, and red carried on with minor hue changes.

As it had done before, Mitsubishi had brought out a model that was a noticeable improvement on its predecessor. You could have been forgiven for thinking that there must be an end to the constant roll of evolution that made each new incarnation of the Lancer so much better than the one it replaced, but if there was a point of no improvement, it wasn't in sight just yet. It was interesting to speculate what the boffins might come up with for next time.

Evolution VI

After shocking everyone with just how good they could make a car in the shape of the Evo V, Mitsubishi wheeled out a new model just one year later. The VI arrived in January 1999, and was the first Evo to retain exactly the same dimensions, power, and torque outputs as the one it replaced. But there were plenty of areas where the new car was nevertheless a definite step forward.

After the quantum leap taken by the body of the Evo V from the IV, the changes to the VI were much more low-key. Mitsubishi had to make all the amendments to the car in accordance with the new WRC regulations that had come into force, limiting the size of all aerodynamic add-ons. This meant some subtle changes to the front and rear aspects. The result of these changes improved the car's performance even though the regulations were more strict than they had been.

The new bumper/grille assembly benefited from the relocation of the number plate, allowing more air to get through to the intakes that fed the radiator and intercooler. The squared plate now squeezed into the gap between the air intake and the relocated fog lights, which were fitted with covers designed to present an easier shape for air to slip around. The fog lamps themselves were smaller than those previously used, in order to allow sufficient room for the number plate. The aperture left open on the driver's side of the bumper fed air to the engine oil cooler, and there was a new outlet vent in the side of the bumper to increase airflow across the oil cooler, raising its effectiveness.

Further work was done to improve engine cooling by fitting a new sump and redesigning the water jacket to help the flow of coolant around the block without it suffering from cavitation. The new sump had different baffling built into it and, together with the new forced-air fed oil cooler that gave 23 per cent better heat dissipation, oil temperature at high engine loadings was stabilised.

While the front-end work was fairly obvious, the side skirts were left untouched. But the rear wing was heavily re-engineered, with two blades to make up for the decrease in size called for by the new regulations. Although the wing was smaller overall, the new design produced just as much downforce as before, and the overall drag figure dropped back to Cd 0.30 as it had been on the Evo IV, even though high-

Opposite: The subtle differences between V and VI aren't easy to spot, but they're there if you look hard enough. The front bumper/spoiler was a new moulding to improve airflow through the engine bay and intercooler. Relocating the numberplate to one side helped enormously.

The Evo VI's rear wing was reduced in size but increased in complexity to circumvent tighter rally regs. The new design was smaller but worked just as well as the Evo V's spoiler, and there was a slight decrease in overall drag, too.

speed stability was better than ever. What's that saying about how the more that things change, the more they stay the same?

Completing the altered look of the Evo VI were new 15-spoke alloy wheels from OZ Racing. These were the same size as those on the last car and they used the same size tyres as well, but the rest of the suspension had been under closer scrutiny and changes were made to raise handling levels even further. At both ends the suspension arms were made from forged aluminium, to improve strength while reducing weight. Roll centre optimisation again increased tyre contact on the road, and the forged components increased rigidity without suffering any weight penalty.

Above: With the new biplane wing format the high-level brake light became very discreet.

Above: Blue-faced instruments were a feature of the Evo VI, and the blue theme was repeated all round the cabin.

Alongside this increased suspension performance, the body was further stiffened by an additional 130 spot welds, and thicker steel was employed in certain areas of the shell, particularly around the front strut mounts. Stronger structural adhesive was also used to improve the strength of the monocoque.

Although the power output hadn't gone up – well, on paper at least – detail changes had been carried out to improve the motor's reliability and response. The new lighter weight pistons also featured oil cooling channels to increase their tolerance to the pain meted out by the forced induction. Turbo breathing was overhauled too, and a larger air intake pipe was fitted. The GSR used the same model of turbocharger as the Evo V, but the RS was offered with a brand new TD05HRA-16G6-10.5T that was fitted with a titanium alloy turbine to decrease lag and increase response – a world first.

To make whoever drove the Evo VI know that they were in the new version, the interior contracted a case of *Changing Rooms*-itis. New black and blue Recaros were fitted, and blue stitching was used on the gearknob, the gear lever gaiter, and the Momo steering wheel (which was the same one as fitted to the V). New instrument faces followed the blue theme, and also helped to reinforce the feeling that this was a totally different car from the V, even though it was a very similar driving environment.

To go with the new model were new colour choices that saw the disappearance of the yellow option and the return of two shades of blue to go with the white, black, and silver. A total of 7,000 Evo VI RSs and GSRs were sold during the model's lifespan, and the opinion of such press as drove the car was that it was indeed a step up from the Evo V, and one that was well worth getting hold of.

Only six months after the first Evo VI had gone on sale, Mitsubishi brought out the Lancer Evolution Limited. This vehicle differed from its stablemate in having an assortment of Ralliart goodies bolted onto it. A new air filter, induction pipework, and a sports exhaust were the main additions to the spec, and new oil filler and radiator caps made sure anyone looking under a Limited's bonnet knew there was something special going on. Sold only in the Tokyo Bay area, but in familiar GSR and RS variants, the Limited was only 100,000 yen (roughly £530) more expensive than the regular Evo VI. This price proved to be quite a saving on the cost of the added Ralliart bits if they'd been purchased separately, and the cars sold out quickly.

It was to be another six months before enthusiasts would have another new Evo to purchase, but when it arrived it was particularly special.

Opposite: The Evo VI interior sported lots of detail changes over its predecessors but it was largely the same. If it ain't broke, don't fix it!

Lancer Evolution VI Tommi Makinen Edition

To celebrate Tommi Makinen's fourth consecutive World Driver's Championship win in 1999, Mitsubishi introduced the rather long-windedly named Lancer Evolution VI Tommi Makinen Edition. Makinen's feat was indeed remarkable, and one well worth celebrating, particularly as Mitsubishi had a few new tricks they wanted to get onto the Evo before the new model came out the following year.

The most noticeable difference between the Evo VI and what was known in some circles as the Evo VI½ was the front bumper moulding. This had been modified by removing the fog lamps and adding a new vent to feed colder air into the air filter area of the engine bay. The whole profile of the bumper was changed to further improve aero performance and it looked quite a bit more aggressive than the VI's snout.

The suspension and steering had also been tweaked with tarmac-stage use in mind, rather than for rough forest tracks. This comprised lowering the car another 10mm (0.39in), and then optimising its front and rear roll-centres to match. The steering ratio was quickened to aid point-and-squirt cross country dashes, and a three-point strut brace was fitted as standard.

Under the bonnet there were a few new wrinkles, but they were designed to improve the way the motor produced power rather than just increase the outright power figure, already pegged at the Japanese 280PS (276bhp) maximum. Following on from the Evo VI RS's use of a titanium-bladed turbo, the Makinen GSR got one too.

The new TD05HRA-15GK2-10.5T twin-scroll turbo had a smaller compressor wheel and the blade profile was altered to improve the turbo's response. The RS variant was still available with its old turbo, but the GSR's new unit was offered as an option.

In an effort to make the Makinen quieter and more efficient a new exhaust system was specified. This had a sports silencer with a big-bore tailpipe that not only lessened back pressure, but reduced noise as well.

If the engine seemed to be quieter, the exterior of the Passion Red Makinen Edition was certainly louder than any Evo that had gone before. For a small fee of 20,000 yen (around £110) the car could be treated to a decal set that made it a convincing replica of the real rally car. This illusion was enhanced by the use of the same Enkei 17in alloy wheels that were used on the competition version. Standard on the GSR, the Enkeis were an option on the RS model.

To go with the red exterior, the same colour turned up all over the interior furnishings. The upholstery had red inset panels and a 'T. Makinen' logo stitched into the covers of the front Recaros, while the Momo steering wheel, gearknob, and gaiter were all stitched with red thread. And just in case you forgot what you were driving – as if you could – the instruments were swapped to black faces with red numerals. For those who didn't want to drive round in a car reminiscent of the Marlboro fag packet that competed in rallies, the Makinen Edition was also available in white, silver, black, and blue, but the interior was still red-trimmed regardless of exterior colour.

Tommi Makinen was apparently very impressed with the car that bore his name, proclaiming it 'Not only highly efficient, but easy to control and fun to drive too.' Well, with his level of control skills he'd probably be able to pilot a fridge on rusty castors round a rally stage quicker than most of us could manage in a car, but it was nice of him to say such encouraging things about the special.

Above: From the rear, the Tommi Makinen version looked like a purely cosmetic job on an Evo VI featuring new rims. Which wasn't the case at all. (Martin Vincent)

Left: A totally new front end was fitted to help cold air feed into the filter area, and to allow as much air as possible to hit the intercooler core. The deletion of the front fog lamps gave a bit more space to play with. (Ralliart Europe)

Following page: Not all Makinens are bright red on the outside, but they are all red-trimmed on the inside. You're never likely to forget what you're driving when in a Makinen.

Production numbers for the EVO VI½ were limited to 2,500, and a model of the car mounted on a wooden display plaque accompanied each vehicle when it was delivered to its first owner. I wonder how many of them were passed on when the Evo went up for resale? I've seen plenty of Makinens, but no models...

The Makinen Edition was the final incarnation of the second-gen Evolution, but a new model was on the horizon for the new millennium.

Chapter **Four**

Evolution VII and VIII: seventh heaven

Evolution VII

When the Lancer Evolution VII arrived in January 2001, it was a case of 'a little bit more' in all departments. Obviously, one major change was that it was based on the new Cedia model which had been launched the previous May. But underneath that was another refinement of the already successful Evo formula.

To rally nuts and non-enthusiasts alike, the VII probably didn't look quite as menacing as a V or VI, and the flared arches and sculpted snout were more blended in, so they didn't look quite as extreme as those on the models that had gone before. Not only did the new Evo seem a little less sharp, it also looked a lot bigger, although a tape measure would show that the overall length had only increased by 105mm (4.09in) and the height by 45mm (1.76in). But even though it was only a little bit longer and a little bit taller, it looked to some like the Evo was getting a bit too big and sensible as it grew up. Interestingly enough, Mitsubishi thought that the new look was much more chiselled and aggressive, so I suppose menace is in the eye of the beholder.

As you might expect, as the vehicle got larger so it got heavier, adding another 40kg (88.2lb) over its immediate predecessors. And according to the figures released with the car, the power output stayed right on the 280PS (276bhp) limit. Torque did go up, but the few extra Nm – now 382Nm (282lb ft) instead of 373Nm (275lb ft) – was achieved 500rpm further up the rev band.

But just looking at the fact that the Evo had become a little podgier didn't tell anything like the whole story. A quick check of some of the less obvious improvements showed that Mitsubishi's engineers hadn't gone soft: they'd just been working away at making the whole car a better package than before.

There's more power in there?

Even though the 4G63 motor's power output hadn't been raised (officially) the turbocharger had been tweaked to give a wider torque plateau. This meant that 349Nm (257lb ft) was available all the way from 2,750 to 5,500rpm, giving improved driveability and requiring less downshifting to find a decent dollop of power. Over the seven different Evolution incarnations, this engine's power output had risen from 250PS (246bhp) at 6,000rpm to 280PS (276bhp) at 6,500rpm, and the torque from 309Nm (227lb ft) at 3,000rpm to the previously-mentioned 382Nm (282lb ft) at 3,500rpm.

Breathing improvements were instigated all the way through the Evo's inlet and exhaust systems, starting with a 20mm (0.78in) thicker intercooler core that had a different fin pitch to improve the flow of cooling air through it. The end tanks were also redesigned for better charge flow. To aid the intercooler further, the water spray system was uprated, adding another delivery nozzle and giving the driver a choice between manual or automatic spray control.

Following on from the intercooler improvements, the new inlet manifold and port layout was claimed to reduce inlet air resistance by up to 20 per cent. On the other side of the motor a straighter exhaust system, a higher-flow cat, and a dual-mode silencer all did their bit to let the spent gases get out faster. The silencer was fitted with a variable back-pressure valve which helped to cut noise at moderate engine speeds, but dropped back-pressure once the revs rose. Like the Evo VI it had just superseded, the VII was offered with two turbocharger variants depending on whether it was an RS or GSR version, and the difference was the turbine material – Iconel on the GSR and titanium alloy on the RS.

More torque wasn't the only target that Mitsubishi was aiming for when it did the engine makeover, as the whole of the top end was lightened too. The aluminium rocker covers were swapped for die-cast magnesium items, and the camshafts were hollowed out. In addition, the inlet pipes were made from aluminium in an effort to improve steering responsiveness by reducing the moment of inertia at the top of the motor. It might seem like a small point to anyone driving on the road, but when a company that's as dedicated to getting things right as Mitsubishi focuses on a problem like this, it's going to put it right.

While it was busy refining and fettling the motor to work harder, Mitsubishi also added a few improvements in the oil cooler system to give a wider safety margin when the engine was being stressed by enthusiastic driving. A thicker core was employed to give up more heat to the air flowing through it, and extra vents in the

The new Evo's nose was covered in just as many intakes and grilles as before, even if the rest of the body had mellowed a little with age. And those integral headlamps gave tremendous illumination without the need for auxiliary lamps.

bumper moulding allowed that hot air to get away from the oil cooler faster.

Getting the power down

Eking more and more power from a motor is all very well and good, but it's useless until it can all be applied to the road with control and safety, particularly in a rally car. So, even though the engine had been tuned for a bit more torque, the Lancer's transmission was given a thorough revamp to make it even more capable.

To pass the extra beef through to the gearbox the new clutch used an uprated cover with a higher clamp load, together with a larger-diameter centre plate and flywheel. To negate the effect the bigger flywheel and clutch unit would have on the engine's pick-up speed, the components had been redesigned to reduce rotational inertia. The end result was a clutch that

Opposite: Bigger all round, the Evo VII lost some of the aggression of the V and VI, but that snout still had plenty of overtaking presence when it appeared in a rear-view mirror.

Above: This view emphasises how long the cabin is in relation to the car's overall length. The simpler rear wing might not look as impressive as the earlier versions but it works better, improving stability and traction through a wider range of diving conditions. Ain't progress grand?

Below: The beefy standard intercooler can flow lots of air and doesn't need upgrading until big horsepower figures are on the horizon. You can just see the intercooler water spray jets under the bumper lip.

Above left: The automatic Evolution GT-A looks a lot more restrained than its manual-transmissioned brother, but it could open up Evo ownership to a new group of enthusiast drivers who have always thought that the radical Mitsubishi might be a little too focused for them.

Above right: This vent is an outlet for the air flowing across the oil cooler hidden inside the bumper. Just like its predecessors, every bit of an Evo has purpose.

could handle the extra power without any problems, and one that remained user-friendly.

The five-speed gearbox was treated to some stronger steel gears that would increase durability under high-load situations and improve the unit's all-round reliability. The first-gear ratio was also lowered to improve standing start acceleration. Top gear was also altered, to take into account the extra torque the motor was now delivering, allowing less revs at motorway cruising speeds with the welcome added benefit of marginally better fuel economy. 'Better' being a relative term to an Evo owner...

Following on from the gearbox's overhaul, the transfer box was uprated to improve longevity. The

gears throughout the unit were uprated and it was now fitted with tapered roller bearings. The case was strengthened by the addition of reinforcing ribs that were cast into it. The propeller shaft, universal joints, and driveshafts also got the once-over, taking them up to motorsport levels of reliability.

The major focus of this work was the change from the earlier cars' viscous centre differential to the new computer-controlled Active Centre Differential (ACD) that used a multi-plate clutch. Not only did this unit rely on interpreting information from a bank of sensors fitted around the vehicle to figure out how to manipulate the centre diff, it did it taking into account the setting chosen by the driver on a three-position switch on the dash. This allowed a choice between 'Tarmac', 'Gravel', and 'Snow' settings, which the computer then used to alter the ultimate amount of diff lock that could be applied to the centre unit. This control also gave experienced drivers the chance to drive with supposedly the wrong setting – such as using 'Gravel' when on wet tarmac – to improve performance. The final tweak was that the diff unlocked when the handbrake was used to initiate tight turns by locking the rear wheels.

Although these BBS rims aren't standard on the Evo they suit it down to the ground . . .

Opposite: Well, we haven't seen one for a while.

To stop any unnecessary additional weight creeping on to the Evo chassis, the new ACD shared the computer and actuation equipment used by the AYC, saving the need to double up on componentry. Together with the Sports ABS, Mitsubishi referred to this package as the All-Wheel-Control system.

Nice suspenders

Although the body of the Evo VII was completely new, the suspension layout was very similar to that of the outgoing model. However, the MacPherson strut front and multi-link rear set-ups had been extensively rejigged to fit in with the increased chassis size of the new car, and there were numerous benefits for ride and handling that were due to the increased dimensions.

The front track was increased by 5mm (0.19in) up to 1,515mm (59.09in) and the roll-centre height was changed to improve cornering performance from initial turn-in through to the limit. The suspension bump stroke travel was also increased by 15mm (0.59in) to 90mm (3.51in). To give greater linearity in the front toe settings, the steering gearbox was lowered, and this also increased vehicle stability during turns. Additionally, a flatter-section cross member and a lower two-point brace increased the stiffness of the front suspension, aiding steering feel and decreasing roll in high-G cornering. The strut towers were linked by a three-point bar that transferred suspension loading into the centre of the bulkhead at the rear of the engine bay, further helping to solidify the front end.

At the rear end of the Evo the track had been increased too, bringing it up to 1,515mm to match the front set-up. As well as increasing the bump stoke on the rear dampers, they were uprated along with the springs and suspension bushes. The roll-centre height was also tweaked in line with the front end, with the overall result that the car was better balanced all the way through its cornering performance.

Finishing off the GSR model's suspension package was a new design of 17in alloy wheel that was shod with high-grip Yokohama Advan rubber in a suitably chunky 235/45/ZR17 size. As usual with the more motorsport-orientated RS version, the steel rims with 205/65/R15 rubber were still standard issue. Obviously, if the car was being bought for competitive off-road use, the owner would have plenty of rims and tyres to choose from, depending on event and conditions. As standard, the RS came with smaller brakes to fit behind the smaller wheels but, if the owner went for the 17in rims, there was the option to go for the 320mm Brembo set-up.

Go faster, stop faster

After this great long list of improvements designed to get the flying Mitsubishi from A to B faster than ever before, it's probably about time we considered the braking system. Already massively powerful, the Evo VII system used the same Brembo calipers and discs that were carried over from the Evo VI, but in conjunction with an uprated master cylinder. The Sports Anti-lock Brake System now used Electronic Brake Force Distribution to give the best compromise of braking effort and handling under any given circumstance.

As well as reading speed information from the road wheel, and lateral and longitudinal G sensors, a new steering angle sensor let the brake ECU know when the steering wheel was turned. Having monitored all the relevant signals from around the car, the ECU

DID YOU KNOW?

In case you were wondering exactly what Cedia means, it doesn't mean anything really. It just comes from combining the first bits of Century and Diamond. Thank goodness Mitsubishi stuck to the Lancer name for the Evolution version.

Proving that they could keep their eye on two differing requirements, the engineers also made sure that the Evo VII's exhaust output was clean enough to pass the Japanese 2000 Emission regulations. This was achieved mainly through the use of a new exhaust gas recirculation valve and a larger capacity catalytic converter. It's so nice to know that when you're driving an Evo and having just about as much fun as you can on four wheels, you can almost be doing your bit for the planet as well.

Smart new Momo steering wheel doesn't look as cumbersome as the outgoing model, but still has the airbag. Note how the trim ring theme is echoed on the gearlever surround, too.

apportioned braking effort around the wheels to give the maximum required retardation in the most stable way. The result was that an Evo VII could complete a corner on the chosen line without losing control if the brakes were applied.

To combat any possible brake fade problems during high-stress situations, the Evo's front under-tray was fitted with ducting that forced cooling air into the brake caliper area of the wheel. As well as keeping the brake performance within safe limits, this also had the useful by-product of extending pad life.

The upshot of all the chassis work, together with the slight increase in torque and the stiffer bodyshell, was a car that Mitsubishi reckoned surpassed even the dynamic performance of the Evo VI Tommi Makinen

Edition. Reports of better handling stability, less understeer, and more accurate and tauter response, together with higher cornering limits, were all touted as improvements on the Evo VII. No doubt the integrated control of the ACD and AYC systems helped out, along with the wider track and stiffer bodyshell, and the new wheel and tyre package.

The body beautiful?

Although still pretty obviously a Lancer Evolution, the VII seemed much bigger and softer than the V or VI that had gone before. While Mitsubishi was trying to tell everyone that the new car looked more aggressive than the older ones, there was something about it that seemed almost middle-aged by comparison. It certainly seemed to frown more. Having said that, the new clothes had been arrived at through sensible design requirements. The short nose with its pared-down corners was used to improve visibility and manoeuvrability, while the integrated lamp units offered better beam distribution and an increase in light intensity. This illuminated a wider field of view, making for safer night driving. And having the lights in one package at the top corners of the front end meant more room for cooling scoops and vents.

The front bumper was given multiple vents to allow the necessary airflow to get to the radiator, oil cooler, and intercooler, while the bonnet vents were designed to quickly drag the warmed air out of the engine bay and keep the motor happy. The bumper moulding also assisted with the aerodynamic performance by directing air away from the underside of the car, decreasing lift and drag.

The Evo VII GSR's twin-DIN radio allocation can be used for two stereo head units or like this, where one slot now houses an auxiliary power meter.

The new Evo VII's instrument panel gives prominence to the tachometer, complete with Active Centre Diff readout. Third fastest-moving needle belongs to the fuel gauge which plummets with sickening rapidity.

The new aluminium front wings bulged out with integral pulled arches rather than the add-on types of the previous models. This saved weight and looked less noticeable, and the rear arches were blended into the back doors to improve the airflow around the Evo's tail. The new spoiler design still looked pretty outrageous, but it had been modified by the removal of the boot-lid mounted wicker to save weight. The wing element was larger than before and had been tweaked for improved downforce. As a result the spoiler helped both straight-line stability and cornering performance by reducing rear-end lift, so improving traction.

The totally new interior was very simple, but gave prominence to all the tools necessary to get the job of driving quickly done with the minimum of distraction. The new airbag-equipped Momo steering wheel looked pretty classy, and the centre ring design was continued on to the gear lever surround. The dash layout gave pride of place to the large tachometer, which – on the GSR model – was also fitted with the ACD status indicator. There were no other engine gauges like oil pressure or temperature, but when you're driving quickly you should be watching the road rather than trying to assimilate too much information coming from the dashboard. The small speedo did take a longer glance than was ideal, particularly if you wanted to check you weren't having too much fun for the boys in blue.

To keep the driver and front-seat passenger comfortably located, a pair of Recaro seats similar to the Evo VI's was used. But even the seats had caught

the Evolution bug, and these new ones had been pared down by 3kg (6.6lb) each, while still providing exceptionally comfortable and precise occupant location. The trim material was changed to a rather subdued blue/grey tweed inset with a black surround. Blue stitching was carried through the rest of the interior furnishings to tie everything together cosmetically.

Externally the Evo VII was offered in a wider colour palette than any Evo before. A dark grey pearl had joined the more usual combination of blue, red, yellow, white, black, and blue. To make up for this surfeit of colours, the RS remained available in white only. As the Evos had become more sophisticated, so the option list had lengthened. It was now possible to buy all the GSR bits for the RS, plus a few uprated suspension parts that would improve the car's track manners even further.

It was interesting that while Mitsubishi thought the car an aggressive and logical step forward on the Evo ladder, some enthusiasts considered it softer because of its larger size and smoother body. However, Japanese touring car diver Takayuki Kinoshita reckoned that although the Evo VI was a wilder ride, the Evo VII would ultimately prove faster in the hands of anyone who didn't have years of race experience. Maybe being a little softer and more developed was better after all.

Whatever Mitsubishi says, the proof of how good a car the Evo VII is can only be found behind the wheel. I really enjoyed hurtling around in one when I got the chance, and even though I didn't get too much opportunity to make reams of notes about how it compared to other Evos I'd experienced, it certainly felt very quick and very controllable over some less than perfect road surfaces, as well as being deceptively speedy under motorway cruising conditions. Even though you spend most of your time watching other traffic like a hawk, and looking at the rapidly approaching horizon, you need to keep flicking down to the speedo just to check how much danger your licence is in...

Automatic for the people – but which people?

Before we move on from the Evo VII and take a quick look at the very latest Evolution, we have to mention the Lancer Evolution VII GT-A, which is something of an oddity in the rally-bred world. While most enthusiasts can see the point of refining a car over a series of

The new **Recaro** seats have kept up with the Evolution's constant tweaking and are even lighter than the ones fitted in the last version. Trick material feels grippy and comfortable and does its best to stop the driver getting all hot and bothered.

DID YOU KNOW?

The Evo VIII is the first homologated Evo ever offered to the American market, but it's somewhat stripped down for our transatlantic cousins. It doesn't have Super AYC (Active Yaw Control) or ACD (Active Centre Differential) and it doesn't get the six-speed gearbox we do either. Nice to know we're not the poor relations all the time.

Whatever the reason behind the new variant, the gearbox wasn't the only thing that had been changed. The most obvious differences were the changes between the exterior features, specifically the bonnet and rear wing. In an effort to reduce air resistance – and give an exterior that was 'more refined and more matured' – the bonnet vents were deleted, as were those in the front bumper. At the other end the large variable-angle wing was replaced with a much more discreet item that held a high-level brake light. There was even the factory-option to do away with the spoiler completely.

Moving to the interior, things didn't seem that unlike the manual-gearbox version until you looked closely. Obviously the gear lever was slightly different with its straight shift pattern, but the Momo steering wheel and gearknob had gone, and the dash had changed to a three-dial layout. The new steering wheel gained a couple of gearshift buttons that would allow a driver to keep both hands on the wheel and still shift up and down the 'box without resorting to the gear lever or leaving the 'box to sort things out for itself.

Another concession to comfort was the installation of larger sports seats instead of the Recaro hip-huggers offered in the GSR. These were still available as an option, as was leather trim for those who really wanted that extra touch of luxury. Interestingly it was noted that the seats were fitted slightly higher than in the regular VII to make getting in and out a bit easier. For anyone who would really struggle with seating as low as the sports seats, the optional leather chairs were mounted even higher.

To accompany these comfort increases, Mitsubishi's engineers also set about reducing noise levels by adding more soundproofing and altering various components so that they wouldn't offend the more delicate ear of the mature buyer the car was aimed at. Steel intercooler piping silenced the high-frequency part of the intake noise, a choke in the exhaust reduced the burble, and the sump was made from steel to damp vibration.

models to make it a little less raw-edged and a bit more user-friendly, the arrival of the GT-A with its five-speed automatic transmission was greeted with a few raised eyebrows.

Mitsubishi's reasoning behind the new model was to make the Evo VII's exceptional dynamic performance available to a wider audience, while its GT-A designation reflected the car's grand tourismo character. I'm sure plenty of would-be drivers might have said the way to widen the Evo's audience was to reduce the price so that more people could afford the cars already being built...

Having made the interior a nicer place to be, the engine was 'matched' to the automatic transmission. This meant maximum power dropped slightly to 272PS (268bhp) at 6,500rpm and torque went down to 343Nm (253lb ft) at 3,000rpm.

The INVECS-II Sport-Mode 5A/T automatic gearbox was brought in from the Galant VR-4, and was a very sophisticated piece of kit. It could be used as a pure auto – you just engaged D and let the 'box do the thinking for you – or in manual operation form, allowing the driver to shift up and down through the gears either with the steering wheel buttons or with the lever. If the latter method of gear selection was chosen the computer still looked over the driver's shoulder, and if a down-change was attempted that might over-rev the motor it would be blocked. An audible alarm would also sound to let the driver know that he'd tried something that wasn't too bright – 'keeping him in closer touch with the operating status of his vehicle', as Mitsubishi opined.

Apart from the auto 'box and the mildy-detuned motor, the GT-A also had softer suspension to give a more compliant ride. The sales blurb even went as far as to say that: 'the GT-A's flatter ride and more natural bump stroke give the driver more control when driving fast on winding roads.'

Summing up the GT-A is a bit difficult. It seems to have been put together to appeal to the sort of driver who wasn't drawn to the regular Evo because it was too much to put up with on a daily basis. But by being quieter, a little less frantic, and less edgy, the whole Evo experience is diminished. On the other hand, if money and garage space were no object, I'm sure a few diehard Evo enthusiasts would be persuaded to give a GT-A some room for those days when getting to their destination could be taken at a slightly easier pace, and without getting quite so breathless along the way.

Ten years on, and another Evolution

Released to the public in April 2003, the Lancer Evolution VIII has been tweaked in the customary way to give a little bit more of everything – again.

Knowing that Mitsubishi's engineers can keep on getting minute improvements out of original designs that were put together some years previously, I'm almost waiting for the day when Mitsubishi announce a 500bhp car that weighs next to nothing, carries six passengers in comfort but without compromising handling, is totally rigid but sticks to the road like it's wearing Velcro tyres, and costs less than a Mars Bar! How's that for Evolution?

Ridiculous author flights of fancy aside, the VIII has been treated to plenty of detail changes to give it another slight edge in performance over its predecessor. It's also been back to the styling studio and come out looking much more aggressive than the softened VII. The added bonus is that those body mods have helped improve the aerodynamic performance too. The nose has come in for the most obvious attention, growing 35mm (1.37in) in the centre, but losing bulk from the front corners. This was done to make visibility better and aid the car's positioning during spirited driving.

While plenty of time was spent in Mitsubishi's wind tunnel facility, a lot of testing was done at the Nürburgring, so the improvements really are fully road-tested before release. Sounds like quite a job doesn't it, screaming round the 'Ring all day and then going out and doing some more the day after? I suppose there are worse occupations...

The main areas that have benefited from the aerodynamic work are engine and charge cooling, and downforce. The trademark vented bonnet has been redesigned with the main vent further forward and some 60 per cent larger than on the VII, and a small lip on the front edge of the vent to give a larger amount of negative pressure over the hole, to drag the hot air out. The small NACA duct that used to be fitted on the left-hand side of the bonnet has now been deleted, lowering drag as well as allowing the main vent to be larger in line with WRC regulations. To further reduce drag over the front of the vehicle, the radiator intake vents in the front bumper have been made smaller, but the larger extraction vent seems to make up for that. While the small intakes have been reduced, the large lower intake has been increased in size to let more cool air get through to the intercooler, raising its efficiency.

The final front-end mods are based around the engine oil cooler and the way air gets to it. The cooler is mounted at the right-hand end of the bumper with a new duct that promotes smoother airflow through the small oil radiator, and this means the side air vent has been dispensed with, as has the matching opening in the left-hand end of the bumper. These small mods have further reduced frontal drag.

What you can't see from a straight-ahead look at the VIII is the amount of airflow direction management that's going on under the front end. Not content with the VII's ducting that forced cooling air towards the brakes, the new front under-tray increases downforce as well as helping with transmission component cooling. Without going too far into the aerodynamic science of

The Evo VIII has an even pointier snout than the VII, and the biggest bonnet vent ever fitted to an Evo. It seems amazing that every Evo continues to get more efficient at going fast than the previous one, but they seem to manage to do it.

the design, this new under-tray has a small airdam along the front edge which increases the negative pressure under the car, effectively sucking it closer to the ground. A cavity immediately behind the airdam multiplies this effect, and then a venturi tunnel speeds up the airflow under the car and increases the effect again, particularly at higher speeds.

Once the air has whipped through these downforce aids, a diffuser splits up the airflow and directs it into separate streams that head toward the brakes, transfer case, and gearbox. The diffuser also slows the airspeed down so that while the cooling effect on these vital components is enhanced, there is no additional drag penalty.

At the back end of the VIII, the boot spoiler has been subtly redesigned from the VII's version, so that it now works better and weighs less. This is the first time a full carbon fibre-reinforced plastic wing has been used on a four-door saloon like this, and even though

The overall profile of the Evo VIII isn't far removed from the VII, but the details are there if you look closely. The carbon-fibre rear spoiler increases downforce without raising drag, and the whole car looks a bit more purposeful than the one it replaces.

the side supports are painted body colour, underneath they are also carbon fibre. By using this material instead of either ABS or aluminium as on previous cars, the new wing has been made slimmer but, by cunningly moving it towards the rear of the car, it now sits in a faster airstream. This means the downforce provided by the spoiler alone is improved to almost twice that of the earlier models, while there is no increase in drag – proof you can have your aerodynamic cake and eat it, as long as you're good in the wind tunnel. These improvements have come about even though the new spoiler design complies fully with WRC regs by being non-adjustable. This, together with the new material, also means it is 2kg (4.4lb) lighter than before.

These small tweaks to the Evo VIII's air management have given the car significantly lower lift and better high-speed handling because of improvements in the balance of front-to-rear aero performance. Oh, and the overall coefficient of drag has dropped by a minuscule

0.01 as well, which, in the world of constant, competitive evolution, still matters.

Engine

While all this detail work was being done to the exterior package of the Evo VIII, the bods in the mechanical shop weren't just sitting twiddling their thumbs. They came up with another bunch of improvements to make the 4G63 motor a tad more torquey than the one fitted in the VII, and somewhat tougher too.

The main focus of the tuning was on the turbocharger itself, making it slightly increase boost pressure through the all-important middle rev-range. This means that the new engine tops out with 392Nm (289lb ft) of torque, and while the maximum power output is still pegged at 280PS (276bhp) there is a little more oomph to draw on between 3,500 and 5,500rpm, which is right where you need it.

To give an added margin of operating safety the engine's cooling system has been uprated with a higher-capacity water pump and larger coolant passages through the turbo itself. The aluminium pistons and forged steel con rods have also been improved, so there should be no problems running the motor hard on the street or at a track session.

The rest of the engine modifications might lead you to think that the 4G63 is getting about as refined as possible because the changes are comparatively small. For this model the exhaust manifold has been made lighter by using thinner-wall tubing, and the air conditioning brackets have been swapped for aluminium ones that weigh 30 per cent less. The valve springs and tensioners have also been whittled down by changing their shape and – in the case of the tensioners – their material too. The use of an aluminium crank pulley hub has further helped lower the overall weight as well as reducing rotational inertia. Now, not only is the engine a little lighter and the strain and friction on the valve train lowered, but the motor should spin up faster and there are benefits to the car's handling characteristics from the lump's lowered centre of gravity.

If the engine work just seemed to be a host of minor tweaks, the amount of work done to the transmission has made up for that. The Evo VIII now uses a six-speed close-ratio gearbox to maximise the way the engine's torque can be utilised. The more motorsport-orientated RS version is still delivered with a five-speeder, but the new 'box is available as an option if so desired. The six new ratios have been chosen carefully to give the best of the previous two five-speed units fitted to the GSR and

RS Evos. This means that first is almost exactly the same as in the Evo VII GSR's five-speeder and emphasises acceleration from rest. Then second through to fourth gear are closer to those from the Evo VII RS's race-proven ultra close-ratio box, and the new fifth ratio is lower than the RS ratio was so that the new one is an optimum match to those before it. The new sixth gear ratio is a bit higher than the VII RS's top gear to give a useful increase in top end performance.

These changes to the gearbox and the ratios mean the VIII is quicker through the gears than the old one, and the longer top gear also has a fuel consumption benefit when the car is cruising on the motorway. Finally the new synchro design on first and second, and the stiffer shift cables, should help with the gearchange speed and robustness. A lift collar stops accidental selection of reverse gear, which is now found between fifth and sixth positions.

For Evo VIII RS models the super-close five-speed gearbox has been uprated to handle the higher torque loadings it will see in the heat of competition by changing the materials used on some of the gears and by reinforcing

Even without a bootlid-covering wicker, the new Evo spoiler works better and causes less drag. That's Evolution for you.

Multi-element headlamps look better, perform better and take up less room than the older units, with separate lower lamps cluttering up the bottom spoiler.

the casing. The clutch on both the GSR and RS has also been improved to make it quieter in operation, and to help the way it releases at higher engine speeds.

As you'd expect from a company that looks to its laurels rather than rests on them, the rest of the sophisticated four-wheel-drive system has received a thorough once-over to keep it at the cutting edge of modern transmission design. The AYC system has been around since the Evo IV, but for the VIII it has morphed into Super AYC and uses a new planetary-gear differential that can transfer twice the torque of the old bevel-gear diff. This change allows the Super AYC to transfer more torque between the rear wheels and so reduce any tendency for the Evo to understeer. The Super AYC can also induce larger yaw moments to increase the car's cornering limits.

The combination of Super AYC, Active Centre Differential, and Sports ABS also benefited from the hours spent pounding round the Nürburgring, and the All-Wheel-Control system has been further tweaked to optimise the way the car behaves in each of the three modes chosen by the driver.

The idea behind the separate ACD and Super AYC systems is that between them they will give the Evo and its driver a higher level of cornering performance with a greater safety margin, and a more linear response when the car is near to its ultimate cornering potential. This is what the systems do during the three stages of cornering:

During deceleration on the approach to the turn the ACD decreases the clutch slip to aid braking effort while the Super AYC transfers some drive torque to the inner wheel, to reduce the car's desire to tuck-in at the start of the corner.

When entering the corner the ACD allows more slippage of the centre differential to improve steering feel and responsiveness, while the Super AYC begins to transfer power to the outer wheel, taking into account the speed and angle of the steering inputs coming from the driver, to keep the car turning correctly.

On the exit from the turn the ACD again decreases the amount of slippage through the diff clutch to improve all-round traction, and the Super AYC lets large amounts of torque through to the outside wheel to counteract understeer and power the car through the bend. The beauty of the system is that all the driver feels is tenacious cornering ability and rock-solid balance through the turns. It feels fantastic to attack corners harder and harder without a murmur from the chassis.

In common with the Evos that have gone before, the Evo VIII RS has a more simple transmission system, losing the Super AYC and retaining just the ACD, which had also been retuned for competition work.

Stronger and stiffer

Even though the Evo VII had been a step forward in torsional stiffness and body strength – you guessed it – those funky little Mitsubishi engineers had been out with the computer models to see where they could improve the foundation of the new version. And although you might think there wasn't much left for them to improve, they found plenty of areas where they could strengthen the steelwork without adding much weight.

One which underwent close scrutiny was the joint between the upper and lower body sections. Reinforcements were added at the bottom of the B pillar, and the rear floor section was completely reworked. Extra strengthening also went on around the strut bar mountings on both strut towers and at the centre bulkhead point where the bar was bolted on. The strut bar was made stronger to stiffen up the whole front end. Other detail points were braced or reshaped, and the rear suspension mounts and wheel arch panels were beefed up in the pursuit of a rigid shell.

The outcome of all this work is a car that reacts more predictably to any suspension or steering inputs, and that allows its suspension to work from a more stable platform. This improves the suspension's reaction to the road, while stopping any unnecessary vibration getting through to the driver and distracting him or her from the job of driving.

To make the most of the stiffer platform, the suspension went through a full makeover with almost every part being optimised. As well as small details like the rear damper rods being made from thicker material, and the rear axle fastening bolts being redesigned to improve camber stiffness, the suspension was also reset to work with the new Yokohama Advan 046 tyres. These are wrapped around Enkei six-spoke alloys that are cast and then heat treated to achieve a strength comparable to a forged wheel, and also to lose weight when

compared to a cast rim. As usual, the RS Evo in five-speed form still rolled out of the factory on 15in steelies, but the six-speed variant wore the Enkeis.

The result of all these tweaks is a car that's another step forward from the VII, but, unusually for a new Evo, hasn't put on any weight as a by-product of its enhancements. In fact, the GSR VIII is almost exactly the same weight as the GSR VII, even though the new car has the heavier six-speed transmission. When fitted with the five-speeder, the RS VIII has actually lost 20kg (44lb) compared to the model it replaces, proving that all that time spent with the computers and weighing scales was well worth it after all.

And on the inside...

A quick look over the VIII's interior wouldn't throw up any surprises from the previous model, but there are lots of detail changes. The simple dash layout continues unchanged, but the speedo is the new 270kph (168mph)

This UK-spec Evo VIII FQ-300 wears discreet badging that no-one stands a chance of reading unless the car's parked. And what does FQ stand for exactly? No-one at Mitsubishi's saying.

Left: UK FQ-300 Evo VIIIs also get special Enkei alloy rims. Ultra strong, lightweight, and easy to clean, they also let plenty of cooling air through to the Brembo brakes.

Below: The Evo VIII FQ-300's engine bay looks surprisingly standard apart from the polished hard pipe feeding into the plenum chamber. There are more mods in there, but they're hidden from view.

Opposite: The Evo VIII's interior looks very similar to the VII's, but the gearlever is different. Not only is it a new knob design - stop giggling - it's attached to a six-speed gearbox.

unit used in the US version. The steering wheel is the same as in the VII, but the stitching has been done with black instead of blue thread. The round trim ring detail carried on to the gear lever surround has been deleted in the VIII, and instead a carbon-fibre 'Evolution' trim plate is fitted on the six-speed cars.

One thing Mitsubishi is very proud of is the new gearknob, which is made of softer plastic and is slightly smaller so that gloved hands can work it more easily. Being leather-trimmed it's still fine to use without gloves, but it shows a certain focus on the part of the engineers when they are optimising a gearknob for competition use, doesn't it?

Natty carbon-fibre badging lets everyone know they're in an FQ-300, while softer knob material stops you bruising your hand while changing gear.

Although they look exactly the same, the VIII's Recaro seats have been tweaked too, with thinner side bolsters that are supposed to provide more comfort without compromising their vice-like grip on their occupants. The centre sections are covered in a blue knitted fabric with a weird dimpled finish that is supposed to be high-grip, but with the bolsters doing such a good job of body location these centre sections could be leather covered in chip fat and you wouldn't slide out during heavy cornering. And mentioning heavy cornering leads us neatly on to...

But what's it like to drive?

Before we go on and eulogise about how good the Evo VIII is, I think it would be a good idea to mention the things that don't work well, or would get on your nerves if you owned the car for any length of time. First off, that new spoiler reflects the high-level brake light something awful at night. Every time you hit the brakes you're distracted by the red light shining in through the back window, and it's very irritating.

Next, er – let me see, there *was* something else. But all I can remember is that fluid rush of power as you accelerate hard, change up at the redline, and drop right onto a fat blob of torque. Then there's the way that as you exit every corner it seems like you could have got round quicker, if only you'd trusted the car to do it or you could have seen what was waiting round the bend. OK, the ride's a bit jiggly on rough roads when you're bimbling behind slow traffic, but that's just a great excuse to get past them at the first opportunity. The quicker you go, the better the ride gets. It's true, but it isn't the sort of thing you could rely on as a defence in a court of law.

And you really should be accelerating through every bend to get the chassis to feel right, but that means you're always tooling along when you perhaps should be taking things a bit easier. The way the car romps up from cruising to 'Jeez we're travelling!' is so addictive you've just got to go and fill the tank again, and get back out and do it some more. At an average of around 15mpg when you're playing, you'll be doing that quite a lot.

In a world full of soft-edged super-minis that have precious little going for them apart from luggage space and fuel economy, the Evo VIII is a glorious piece of kit that flatters your driving, makes you feel like a rally champion, and puts a grin on your face a mile wide. But it can also go so fast they'll have you psych-evaluated before they chuck the book at you and then escort you to the cells. Please get an Evo if you can, but use it with care, and keep an eye out for flashing blue lights...

Chapter Five

The Evos are coming – officially!

Although the grey import scene meant that a good few Evos had already worked their way into the UK, Mitsubishi finally gave in and began genuine imports in mid-1999, starting with the Lancer Evolution VI. This was priced at a not inconsiderable £30,995, but road testers still loved it, regardless of price tag. They seemed to grasp the idea that it was a supercar in all but looks, and it was not only easy to drive to very high levels, it was still something of a bargain for the performance it offered.

It was immediately compared to the Subaru Impreza, but it seemed fans of one car would rarely be won over by the other manufacturer's product. Road tests that compared the two were rarely conclusive about which was better, preferring to do some fence-sitting by saying

that each had its virtues and faults. Personally, I'd take an Evo every time, but that's just me.

After the Evo VI had been available in the UK for almost a year, a new version was announced. This was the RSX, a strange, UK-slanted hybrid that combined a basic RS spec with some GSR goodies so that new owners didn't have to put up with the loss of too many creature comforts. The GSR's ABS and AYC had both been omitted, but Recaro seats had been fitted along with air conditioning, electric windows, and a GSR-type airbagged steering wheel. The RS's steel rims were also

The Lancer Evolution VI eXtreme was offered by Ralliart UK for those who wanted something a little bit more radical than the original Evo VI. Just how fast did these people need to get around?

left back in Japan and instead the RSX wore GSR-pattern OZ 17in alloys and 225/45 tyres. The main reason for bringing this model out seemed to be to entice punters into Lancer Evolution ownership for five grand less than the regular GSR VI.

One thing that had changed when the Evo became officially available in the UK was the top speed, which had previously been limited to 112mph (180kph). Now that the electronic trickery was deleted the Evo could stretch its legs and romp up to the 150mph (240kph) region without too much strain. Everyone knew they were devastatingly quick off the line, but this newfound top end was further proof of just how serious the car was.

The next step in UK Evolutions, announced at the Autosport International show in January 2001, was an upgraded rather than a down-specced version, and had a price tag to match. While the regular Evo VI continued at £30,995, the new Evolution eXtreme demanded a £41,995 cheque to open the door. It needed to be pretty extreme to justify the price hike, but plenty of work had been done by Ralliart UK to improve the car.

The main difference was the increase of horsepower output to 340bhp (345PS), well up on the 276bhp (280PS) of the vanilla version. To get this level of grunt from the 4G63 motor yet another new turbocharger was fitted, along with bigger induction and exhaust systems and a remapped engine brain.

As well as the 60-ish horsepower hike, the eXtreme's torque figure went up from 274lb ft to 303lb ft (410Nm). And to make it as satisfying to drive as any other Evo, the driver found these new peaks at exactly the same revs as on the original version. What made the car even more fun to drive was that 165lb (75kg) had been stripped from the car's weight, improving the overall power-to-weight ratio to 270bhp per ton.

The result of these changes was that the Evo eXtreme could accelerate from 0–60mph (0–96kph) in a flat four seconds, and then continue on to 100mph (161kph) in another six. An even more impressive party piece was that it could accelerate from zero to 60mph and then stop again, all in 6.5 seconds. To put that into some sort of perspective, a sports car like a Porsche Boxster takes that long to hit 60mph, never mind start slowing down again.

Although the extra power was very welcome, it would have been nothing without attention being paid to the rest of the chassis to keep things as controlled and safe as they were on all the other Evos. To this end

new engine mounts had been developed to stop the extra torque reaction from ruining the handling.

Apart from an additional front strut-brace to further stiffen the suspension mountings, the actual suspension system was basically the same as on the Evo VI. The ride height had been lowered slightly in line with its tarmac-biased performance, dropping 28mm (1.09in) at the front and 14mm (0.55in) at the rear. Wheel size was raised to 18in with 225/40 rubber. Larger anti-roll bar links and bushes were also used to upgrade the suspension's responses in keeping with the new performance levels. Uprating the brakes was simply done by fitting better disc pads with Mica heat-shield backing, and using competition brake fluid.

Interior mods were kept to a minimum. A set of four-point harnesses was used to keep front seat occupants firmly in position in the new Recaro sports seats during the sort of manoeuvres the eXtreme was capable of. Apart from that there was a new Momo steering wheel, pedal extensions, and a carbon-look dash trim. It might not have had the sort of luxury you'd expect from a forty-grand motor, but then it did have the performance of something that cost twice the price. It wouldn't be the only Evo to be called eXtreme either, as we'll soon see.

Seeing red

In March 2001 the Tommi Makinen Edition reached the UK, going on sale for £32,995 in blue, black, silver, and white, as well as the £700 cost-option red. In UK form its performance was noted as 4.4 seconds for the 0–60mph dash, and topping out at 150mph (240kph). Again the car wooed the press of the time, and everyone raved about the performance and handling levels being phenomenal.

The only downside they picked up on was its voracious appetite for Super Unleaded and the shortened service intervals of 4,500 miles. It was still cheaper to run than almost any Italian exotic, though, and you could take three mates with you when you went out for a blast. Who needs a Prancing Horse?

And what does FQ stand for again?

It was early 2002 before anything significant happened in the UK Evo market, when the Evolution VII was announced at the Autosport International show. Two versions were launched, the RS-II and the FQ-300. The strangely-monikered RS-II was actually an equivalent of the Japanese-spec GSR rather than the RS, and the FQ-300 was a slightly more powerful version of the VII,

Oh, now that's not fair... The Boys in Blue buy something that can keep up and pull you over almost regardless of what you're driving.

without going as far as the eXtreme spec that would follow soon after.

The RS-II was pitched into the market at £29,995, while the FQ-300 cost £1,500 more for the tuning mods. Quite what the FQ stood for was open to interpretation. With schoolboyish smirks Mitsubishi UK press people said it could be either 'flipping quick', or 'fine quality', but when you'd driven one you knew it was nearer to the first version, but with use of a more colourful expletive.

What you got for your £1,500 was basically an uprated breathing package of cat-back exhaust and high-flow panel air filter. The power output went up to something over 300bhp (304PS) and 300lb ft (406Nm), making for an entertaining drive. Performance of both the RS-II and the FQ-300 was said to be limited to 157mph (252kph), and the 0–60 times were 5.5 seconds and 4.9 seconds. A few carbon-fibre bits on the gear lever surround and the spoiler ends made sure the owner knew the car was a bit special.

There were other UK Evo specials to choose from too, like the Evo eXtreme and Evo eXtreme S built by Ralliart UK, who are now Xtreme Automobiles. As with the earlier Evo eXtreme VI, the Evo VII eXtreme models were more muscle-bound than the regular versions, with the eXtreme S being wound up to almost 360bhp (365PS) and 380lb ft (515Nm) of torque. Hence the name...

DID YOU KNOW?

When it introduced the Evo VI RSX model in May 2000 at a reduced price of £25,995 it seemed that even Mitsubishi wasn't sure if it had a market for such a hybrid. It dipped a toe in the water, making just 30 cars to this spec.

Opposite, top: The Lancer Evolution VII eXtreme S was about as wild an Evo as Ralliart UK could put together. Much more raw and raucous than the regular Evo VII, it was more at home on the track than the road. (Dave Woodall)

Opposite, bottom: Although the Evolution VII eXtreme S didn't have lots of flashy body mods, it was a devastating thing to drive. Most other track-day participants would get to see this rear end aspect as it disappeared into the distance. (Dave Woodall)

The eXtreme was based around fairly straightforward engine durability mods, comprising new conrods and pistons. There was a Ralliart Sports ECU, breathing improvements from a new induction kit and exhaust system, and Group N Roll Stop engine mountings. The clutch was a 25 per cent uprated unit that could handle the raised power output of 338bhp (343PS) and 350lb ft (474Nm) torque, and acceleration was timed at 0–60 in 4.2 seconds. None too shabby. Braking performance was increased with cross-drilled discs, braided hoses, and a brake master cylinder anti-flex kit. Suspension mods consisted of Eibach sports springs to lower the car a little, and then Group N mountings in the steering and suspension.

The eXtreme S was a bit more focused than its little brother, and the basic mods were built upon to get to the final spec. After the motor-strip to swap pistons, con-rods, and camshafts, a ported and polished cylinder head was employed to make the most of the new bigger titanium turbo and uprated intercooler. A programmable electronic brain was fitted to fulfil the new spec's fuel and ignition requirements.

Group N componentry was again used throughout the suspension and steering mountings, but the braking was totally reworked. Massive 362mm AP Racing discs were gripped by six-pot calipers at the front, while the rear discs were swapped for drilled items, and four-pot calipers put on the squeeze. Both eXtreme models were shod with light alloy wheels that went up in size but down in weight. Given the history of Ralliart UK coming up with cars like this, I can't wait to see what they manage to do with the Evo VIII.

The Evolution VII eXtreme S interior shows how single-minded it is, with race harnesses and lighter, more vice-like Recaro seats. (Dave Woodall)

Grey area

It was interesting to note that Mitsubishi took the opportunity to throw some doubt on the validity of grey import cars by stating that all the official cars available in the UK would come with a serial number and a passport to prove they were genuine, and not vehicles with a possibly dodgy history.

Bearing in mind that Mitsubishi in Japan made all the cars, and that an imported car could have a much cleaner bill of health than a used-and-abused UK second-hander, this smacked of sour grapes on the part of the company's UK arm. If Japan hadn't built such a world-beating car in the first place, Mitsubishi would surely have struggled to gain any real credibility in the performance car arena, and might have failed to take any profit from that area of the market at all.

The demand for the cars was there whichever way you looked at it, so badmouthing unofficial imports wasn't going to stop them being sold to enthusiasts who couldn't afford the top-dollar UK model prices. And Japan's draconian vehicle regulations meant that a steady stream of cars needed to find homes in other countries, so why gripe about it?

In a further effort to stifle the grey import market for late models, Mitsubishi took the unprecedented step of launching the Evo VIII in the UK before anywhere else in

The UK-spec Evo VIII is also available in breathed-on FQ-300 form. Small badges give the game away, but who'll get a chance to see them?

Europe, and promised to keep it that way for the first year. The price of the new vehicle was also dropped – £3,000 lower for the regular car and £2,500 down for the FQ-300.

Following on from the Evo VII's lead, the UK-spec VIII was again available in two guises, but the confusing RS-II name had disappeared. Now there was simply the Evo VIII or FQ-300 to choose from, with the performance mods of the FQ-300 being based around the same breathing changes used previously. The recipe seemed to be a winner, because Mitsubishi had 200 orders before the car was available, out of an allocation of 900 units for the year. And again Mitsubishi stressed that because of the improved price and the all-encompassing warranty there was really no need to go and buy an Evo from anywhere else.

And that about brings the Evo story up to date for now. But the story is bound to run and run, especially as the factory WRC team looks set to return to rallying in 2004, and more variations on the theme will arrive as tuners get used to extracting larger amounts of power from the 4G63 motor.

Stick around, it should be quite a ride.

Chapter **Six**

History lesson

Because the focus of this book is aimed at the Lancer Evolution as a road car, we aren't going to go over every rally that an Evo has entered and give you a stage-by-stage breakdown of what happened. There are numerous publications and videos about the World Rally Championship (WRC) that have the time and room to go into that kind of detail, so we'll leave it to them.

What we're concerned with is picking out the highlights – and a couple of sadly unmissable low points – of the Evo years and showing you how the Mitsubishis became stronger, and one driver became a phenomenon in World Rallying. Although we're going to

Armin Schwarz tears up Greek dirt tracks on the 1993 Acropolis Rally, going on to finish third. (Ralliart Europe)

major on Group A (which was the highest level of the sport until the WRC class was announced) there are a few honourable mentions to go to the Group N drivers and those involved in the Asia Pacific Rally Championship (APRC), where Mitsubishi also competed. So, let's go back to 1993, and the dawn of the Evo era.

Group A Lancer, year by year

1993

Having spent years developing the rally cars that preceded the Lancer Evolution, Ralliart brought the new vehicle out for its first taste of competition in January 1993 on the Monte Carlo, ten years after the last Lancer EX2000 Turbo had been driven in the World Rally Championship. Two cars were entered, driven by Kenneth Eriksson with Stefan

Parmander navigating, and Armin Schwarz with Nicky Grist, but both vehicles had some problems that left them in fourth and sixth positions. Even though they weren't without a few teething problems, getting both Evos to the finish was a great start to their career.

The Ralliart cars didn't contest the full WRC, sticking to just seven of the 13 rounds that year, of which five were entries looked after by Ralliart Europe. Armin Schwarz gave the Evo its first podium finish with a third on the Acropolis Rally in Greece, but that was to be the only trophy the car would win until Kenneth Eriksson came away with a second from the RAC Rally. At the end of the year Eriksson was seventh in the Drivers' Championship, while the team were eventually promoted to fourth spot after another manufacturer had its drivers' points removed for one event.

1994

During the off-season Mitsubishi's rally engineers made several tweaks to the car based on the information they'd gleaned from the previous year's exploits. One major problem related to the way the centre differential reacted to the car being airborne and the lack of traction found on landing. This was attended to on the Evo I, even though the Evo II was waiting to be launched later in the year.

The driver team was the same as for 1993, but this time Armin Schwarz was partnered by Klaus Wicha, with

whom he'd worked with at Toyota some years before. Both drivers were extremely quick on the Monte Carlo, but overall inconsistency saw them drop to fifth and seventh by the finish.

Although the Japanese driver Kenjiro Shinozuka finished second on the Safari Rally in March, the Evo I never actually won an event before it was superseded. But the string of podium finishes showed the Evo programme definitely had potential.

The new Evo II was wheeled out for the Acropolis Rally in May. Schwarz drove it to a fantastic debut second place, but his teammate Eriksson went out with broken suspension. The modifications proved worthwhile, though, as the new car was much more stable at high speed thanks to its new front lower spoiler and redesigned boot-lid spoiler.

The New Zealand Rally was an event on both the WRC and APRC calendars, and 1994 saw a third and fourth place pairing for the Group A cars, with Schwarz holding off Eriksson, but after that the WRC season was somewhat disappointing. In the APRC, however, things were looking better. Kenneth Eriksson and his Evo II took two wins in Indonesia and Thailand, Mitsubishi were second in the Manufacturers' Championship, and

Eriksson was second in the Drivers' Championship, just one point behind the winner.

One interesting thing to note is that at the San Remo Rally a certain Tommi Makinen moved from Group N to Group A. Although he didn't finish that particular event, he was set to be one of the sport's all-time greats and he would be getting plenty of attention very soon.

1995

With the regulation changes that forced all teams to run in all WRC rallies, Ralliart Europe stretched its budget by agreeing with Ralliart Germany to nominate the latter's Group N car as the works entry in those events which Ralliart Europe couldn't attend. It was a cost-effective way to compete at every round when the finances weren't buoyant enough to support a full assault on the championship.

WRC technical regulation changes that year centred around a small-bore air restrictor being fitted into the turbocharger to limit the airflow available to the motor. This had the effect of putting everyone on a similar footing by allowing the top teams only around 300bhp to play with. To further improve their cars, Mitsubishi brought in electronically-controlled front and centre diffs for better power distribution. The cars also ran the Post Combustion Control (PCC) system to improve engine response, making up for the limitation posed by the regulation air restrictor.

Beware low-flying Evos! Kenneth Eriksson proves the new aerodynamics on the Evo III don't always manage to keep it firmly on the ground. The photographers should have paid more attention to him, as he went on to win the 1995 Australian Rally. (Ralliart Europe)

From the start the Evo IIs were quick, and Makinen looked set to clinch a third spot on the Monte Carlo until mechanical troubles dropped him to fourth. But, on the Swedish Rally the following month, Mitsubishi won their first WRC event with a Lancer Evolution when Eriksson headed Makinen home for a great one–two. Makinen allowed his team-mate past when he was given orders to let Eriksson win.

Although it wasn't part of the WRC, the 1995 Safari Rally was notable for Kenjiro Shinozuka's Evo II/III. The car he'd been running for two years was updated to Evo III spec and it rewarded him by carrying him to a second place in this notoriously rough event.

The 'genuine' Evo IIIs were wheeled out for the Tour de Corse in May, and Andrea Aghini immediately put one into third place, while Tommi Makinen was racking up more experience by managing eighth place on a rally that he'd never done before.

After a lacklustre performance on the New Zealand Rally where Eriksson could only manage a fifth and Makinen fell off the road, the next round that counted towards WRC honours was held in Australia. Eriksson took first place, with Makinen fourth.

Although the Evos didn't do particularly well at Catalunya, this event was famous (infamous, perhaps) for the Toyota team being caught cheating to get around the power loss imposed by the air restrictor. Aghini took fifth while Makinen again failed to finish, but the points gained at least put Mitsubishi above everyone else in the manufacturer standings.

Sadly this lead was lost on the RAC Rally when both Eriksson and Makinen went out. Instead, Colin McRae became World Champion and Subaru won their first manufacturers' title. At least Mitsubishi did better in the APRC, where Eriksson and Mitsubishi won both driver and manufacturer titles to sweeten the disappointment of the WRC.

1996

This season saw Tommi Makinen start as the only full-programme driver in the Mitsubishi Ralliart Europe team. Richard Burns was signed up to compete mainly in the APRC and Didier Auriol made some guest appearances towards the end of the season. Unlike previous years, the Evolution III was to contest all the events without handing over to its successor halfway through the season. And what a season it turned out to be.

The WRC passed by the Monte Carlo as the eight-event rotation system was used for the last time. This meant the first WRC points-scoring rally of the year was the Swedish, which Makinen won without any problem, having set fastest time on ten of the 27 stages.

Despite breaking a driveshaft on the first day of the Safari Rally, Makinen was back on top of the leaderboard by the end of the second day and he stayed there until the end. It was the first time for more than ten years that anyone had won the Safari at their first attempt. He also beat his former team-mate, Subaru-mounted Kenneth Eriksson, by a whopping 14 minutes. This, combined with the Swedish Rally win, must have been particularly sweet for Makinen, especially after being told to let Eriksson through on the Swedish the previous year.

After a DNF on the Indonesia Rally, Makinen managed a second on the Acropolis to keep him marginally in front of Carlos Sainz in the Drivers' Championship. An easy win in Argentina increased this lead further, and then another on the 1000 Lakes in Finland widened the gap even more. It also moved Mitsubishi ahead of Subaru in the manufacturer standings.

The Australian Rally saw Makinen take another win and bag enough points to make him World Champion for the first time. Things were tighter in the manufacturer league and, although Mitsubishi pulled away from Subaru after the Australian event, Makinen's crash on the next rally in San Remo, and Auriol's eighth place, meant Subaru closed them down. Subaru won its second championship after the Spanish Rally, where Makinen could only manage a fifth place. After Makinen's co-driver Seppo Harjanne was injured in the San Remo crash, Juha Repo had stepped into the hot seat and the pair were a little off the pace.

In the APRC it was a reversal of fortunes when Eriksson retained the drivers' title in his new Subaru, while Mitsubishi won the manufacturer honours following victories for Burns in New Zealand, Makinen in Australia, and Ari Vatanen in the Hong Kong–Beijing Rally.

1997

A major change for 1997 was the dropping of the eight-round rotation scheme. This meant all 14 rounds of the WRC had to be contested. The year also saw the relaxing of the homologation rules to let manufacturers build special cars purely for rallying if they wanted to. This WRC class should have been the top of the tree, but Mitsubishi stuck with the Group A format for their rally challenger and built on the success of the Evolution III.

The Evo IV had been released the previous year, and testing had gone on through to the end of 1996. Because it was a completely new car it couldn't be homologated under the same spec as the Evo I–IIIs, so the Evo IV was homologated as a brand new model on 1 January 1997. Although the Group A spec was much closer to a real road car than a WRC machine, the Evo IV wasn't short on rally-specific toys like a sequential gearbox and water-cooled brakes for the faster tarmac events. And although the Evo IV was fresh out of the box, the previous years of development hadn't gone to waste. Well-tested features like the PCC system and the clever active four-wheel-drive system were carried straight over, with a few tweaks for the new application.

Through the first three events of the 1997 season Makinen struggled to get his car back on top and, although it showed plenty of promise, a win eluded him. Third places in Monte Carlo and Sweden meant he was still in contention, but he was playing catch-up rather than leading from the front.

The Evo IV's first win came on the fourth rally of the season in Portugal, and not only was it the first time that Makinen had got to the top of the podium in the new car, it was the first time a sequential transmission-equipped car had ever won a WRC rally. Makinen was very impressed with the new 'box and gear selection system. It proved its worth by giving him a four-minute lead over second place.

After the dustbowl of Portugal, WRC moved on to the road stages of Spain, where Makinen proved the new car's worth on tarmac by winning again. His lucky streak wasn't to continue on the Tour de Corse, though. A small altercation with a stray cow ended up with Makinen, Harjanne and the Evo going over a cliff. Normal service was resumed in Argentina when Makinen took the top prize with ten stage wins out of 23.

After moving on to Greece for the Acropolis Rally, Makinen and the Evo IV could only manage third position, but Burns and co-driver Robert Reid were there to support the team effort with a fourth place finish. New Zealand was even worse for the Finn when he crashed out and made an awful mess of his car. Burns couldn't repeat his Acropolis form either because of transmission problems.

Coming into the 1,000 Lakes, Makinen was still hanging on to his lead in the Drivers' Championship, and he added to this by winning his home event. That made it four times in a row – a stunning achievement. Indonesia proved to be a bit more of a thorn in his side when he retired, doing nothing for his season's tally.

Although he was hampered by set-up problems on the San Remo Rally, Makinen managed to get the Evo IV home in third place, which, more importantly, meant he

was still ahead of Carlos Sainz, his nearest rival for that year's title.

The Australian event was no easier on the Mitsubishi, with accident damage making the rally an uphill struggle. The amazing thing was that Makinen pressed on to a second place overall and left himself needing just one point from the final event of the year, the RAC Rally held in England. Colin McRae triumphed in Australia, meaning that Subaru won the Manufacturers' crown again – which meant that the best Mitsubishi could hope for was that Makinen would lift the individual title. Although fighting an illness, he finished the RAC in sixth place and scored the point he needed. It was a close-run thing, though, with McRae winning the event to come within one point of Tommi's final Championship-winning tally.

Across the other side of the world the APRC had another year of being dominated by Kenneth Eriksson and his Subaru, giving him the Drivers' title again, and Subaru the Manufacturers' title. Mitsubishis failed to perform to the same level as the Scoobys, but hope was around the corner in the shape of the Evolution V, which would arrive on the scene the following year. Would it fare any better against the Subarus?

In his third year as a Mitsubishi WRC Group A driver, Tommi Makinen gives the Evo IV a good helping of opposite lock on the 1997 Acropolis Rally. The front wing and rear corner show that a little too much enthusiasm on the rough stuff can be damaging. (Ralliart Europe)

The Evo IV was still on the team for the early part of 1998, and here's Tommi Makinen on his way to victory. Note how thin the snow tyres are to cut through the top layer and get the spikes down into the frozen base to give astonishing levels of grip. (Ralliart Europe)

1998

Although the Lancer Evolution IV was running 300bhp (304PS) and 375lb ft (508Nm) by the start of the year, the Evo V was waiting in the wings to take up the fight. It had been on test since the summer of 1997, and would be ready to roll by the fifth event of the 1998 calendar. One of its main advantages was its wider track suspension, which was designed to help it stay on the pace of the WRC cars when rallying on tarmac. Mitsubishi had also made the canny move of homologating two suspension systems – wide and narrow – to allow them to adjust the car for tarmac and gravel rallies.

The year started off with Makinen and his new co-driver Risto Mannisenmaki in the Evo IV making a big impression on the Monte Carlo leader-board, and then on the Monte Carlo scenery as they crashed out of the event. Burns did better by finishing fifth, even though he was on his first Monte Carlo and the weather was foul.

At the next event, in Sweden, the bad luck afflicted Thomas Radstrom, who had led the rally until the halfway point, but on his retirement Makinen was

there to pick up the pieces and keep his first place to the end. Burns wasn't quite so gifted though, as his Stage Two accident dropped him down to 15th position by the finish.

Burns's fortunes were to change on the Safari Rally, where he ran second to Makinen for much of the first two days. When Makinen's car broke its engine mountings Burns cruised through and stayed at the top to take his first Mitsubishi WRC win.

The gremlins that had been chewing away at Makinen took another chunk out of him in Portugal when he hit a tree and retired early. Burns fared better by managing to finish the rally, but a poor tyre choice slowed him down to fourth place.

At the Spanish Rally the Evolution V made its debut, although Burns was again driving one with Carisma GT badges for marketing reasons. Burns had been testing the new car alongside Lasse Lampi during the previous year, but Makinen hadn't had the same time behind the wheel and took a while to get used to the car before he got on the pace. He didn't need very long, considering what he had to concentrate on while he was feeling his way with the new Evo, and he still managed to take third place and stay one position ahead of Burns. It wasn't a bad first outing for the Evo V, so things were looking good for the rest of the year.

Unfortunately, neither driver finished the Tour de Corse Rally, but things did improve on the next event in Argentina, when Makinen won a close battle with Colin McRae after his car broke its suspension. Burns came in fourth to rack up some valuable manufacturer points.

Another electrical fault put paid to any hope of points in Greece, where Makinen went out on the second stage. Burns also didn't manage to finish when his suspension failed just as he was looking good for a top five result. He was also looking pretty good on the New Zealand Rally, when he was in third on the leader-board until he dropped down to 15th on one stage. Although Makinen wasn't on top form he managed to pick up third place, while Burns worked hard to get back up to ninth.

Makinen was back on form for the next round of the WRC in his home country. He also set a new record by winning the rally for the fifth time in succession, and helped his championship hopes by taking the maximum points. This was the first time that Burns had driven in the 1000 Lakes, but even so he managed fifth ahead of much more experienced opposition.

During the gap between the Finnish and San Remo Rallies, the Evo V was fitted with an active electromagnetic clutch in its rear differential to match the two fitted in the centre and front diffs. Using computer control to adapt the power split for all surface conditions and driver commands, the Evolution V was a formidable weapon on any stage. Makinen certainly got on with the new transmission system because he led from the second stage through to the end. Burns didn't catch on quite as quickly as Tommi, but still managed to come home in seventh spot.

Australia was much more to Richard's liking and he was leading until the midway point of the second day, when he was passed by three other drivers. Carlos Sainz was leading the championship going into the Australian event, so getting back near the front was imperative for his title hopes. Makinen and Auriol also passed Burns as they tussled for more points. McRae got into the frame when he went into the lead with two stages left. Sadly for him, his Subaru went pop and so did his chances of winning the Drivers' Championship. But after all the drama Makinen was there to take first place ahead of Sainz. It looked like the title would be decided on the RAC again.

This time it was Burns's turn to impress with a victory over his nearest rival of four minutes. Makinen had gone out early on when his Evo had lost a wheel after an accident. He must have been feeling sick at

having come so close to three consecutive Drivers' crowns when Sainz's Toyota expired close to the finish. That gave Makinen the title after he'd thought he'd already lost it. Burns's points, added to Makinen's, also gave Mitsubishi their first Manufacturers' Championship, making it a very successful season.

While Mitsubishi were flying high in the WRC, things weren't quite so rosy in the APRC. The FIA had decreed that no works' drivers could score points, so it made fielding the top WRC challengers a waste of time. Instead, Mitsubishi put their weight behind Yoshiro Kataoka, who managed to finish second to a Toyota.

1999

Following on from the great 1998 season Mitsubishi rewarded the Evolution V by superseding it with the Evo VI. On the face of it, the new car wasn't any more powerful or any lighter than its predecessor, and FIA regs had limited its suspension development and made it run with a smaller wing. This was redesigned to give the same performance from the smaller area, and the car held its own against the more highly modified WRC cars that had less stringent regs to deal with. In the hot seats were the regular team of Makinen and Mannisenmaki, while new boy Freddy Loix had replaced Richard Burns, who had jumped ship to Subaru. Loix was partnered by Sven Smeets.

Starting as he meant to go on, Makinen led the Monte Carlo Rally more or less from start to finish. Loix, on the other hand, wouldn't want to repeat his crashing out on the first day. In Sweden he at least finished the rally, but down in ninth place. Makinen carried on his winning ways with another top spot, giving him a clear advantage at the head of the Drivers' Championship. As it turned out, he'd need that breathing space to help tide him over an upcoming lean patch.

The Safari Rally was one marked with drama as Makinen was excluded for receiving spectator help when changing a wheel. To make matters worse, Loix had a big accident which not only ruled him out of the Safari, but injured him enough to stop him entering the next event. It wasn't turning into the best debut season for Loix, but he kept trying. As if the exclusion wasn't bad enough, Makinen had actually finished the event in second place, so he lost good points.

To replace the injured Loix on the Portuguese Rally, Mitsubishi drafted in Marcus Gronholm, and he was doing well right up until his Evo's clutch packed up. Makinen struggled with a faulty front differential in the

With its new rear spoiler and exaggerated lamp covers on the front bumper, the Evo VI was easy to differentiate from its predecessor. Tommi Makinen tackles the Acropolis Rally, taking third place on the event and winning the Drivers' title for the fourth time in a row. (Ralliart Europe)

initial stages, but he still managed to drag his car back up to fifth position by the finish.

Loix returned for the next rally in Spain and was rewarded for his steady drive when a jump-start penalty served on Burns promoted Loix to fourth. Unfortunately, Makinen also got a jump-start penalty, and the one-minute addition to his time dropped him down to third. Still, it was more points to add to his total.

Although both Mitsubishi pilots needed to score well on the Tour de Corse, brake problems left them struggling with their cars. Makinen came in sixth and Loix was two places further back. Maybe things would improve in Argentina.

Unfortunately, things *didn't* improve in Argentina. Makinen's gearbox woes caused him to come in fourth, which was still a good result given the problems he'd had en route. Loix crashed out again, but this time without any lasting injuries. At the next event in Greece

both cars scored reasonable points by coming in third and fourth, and Makinen's third place was enough to keep him ahead on the drivers' table. Mitsubishi still weren't getting close to Toyota, though, as the latter kept pulling away in the manufacturers' league.

The New Zealand Rally smiled on Makinen and he went on to win the event with time to spare. Loix only managed to net an eighth position, and the engineers at Mitsubishi considered that they'd really have to make some serious set-up changes to suit Freddy's driving style, rather than make him struggle on with Tommi's set-up.

With the possibility of another straight win on his home 1000 Lakes Rally in the back of his mind, Makinen had to endure transmission problems that dropped him out of the event altogether. Loix did actually complete the event, but collided with some scenery on his way to the finish post, so his tenth place looked quite good.

China's inclusion on the WRC calendar is best not mentioned in front of Mitsi personnel as both cars crashed out, and Didier Auriol now tied with Tommi in the drivers' league. After going into the last stage of the San Remo behind the leader, Makinen won, to get some good points in the bag. Meanwhile the new set-up was

Ralliart Europe

The history of the Mitsubishi Lancer Evolution in competition can't really be told without also telling the story of Ralliart Europe, which was established in the United Kingdom in 1983 by former Mitsubishi driver Andrew Cowan. The idea was that the new company would develop and prepare Mitsubishi cars to participate in the European rounds of the World Rally Championship. This was quite a step forward for the Japanese company, because this new offshoot was the first branch of Ralliart to be formed outside Japan.

Having had several successful years battling the rough and tough rallying terrains of Africa and the South Pacific, Mitsubishi Motors wanted to widen its competition horizons through the diversity of the European circuit. The main problem was one of logistics. Mitsubishi had always prepared rally cars at its Research & Development facility in Japan, which wasn't a good location from which to mount a European campaign. Although the feasibility of expanding into Europe seemed difficult, Mitsubishi had the involvement and encouragement of Andrew Cowan. An added bonus was that the creation of Ralliart Europe would enable Mitsubishi to return the R&D facility to its original use.

The first outing onto the European circuit was the 1989 Rallye Monte Carlo, when Ari Vatanen piloted the Mitsubishi Galant VR-4. Following on from this event, the team competed at the Acropolis Rally in Greece, then the Rally of the 1,000 Lakes in Finland and the RAC Rally of Great Britain.

Although it was thought that the team would run a Group B car to begin with, the Fédération Internationale de l'Automobile (FIA) changed the WRC regulations. Once this happened Mitsubishi and Ralliart Europe were able to enter Group A cars. This was better for Mitsubishi because it meant that the European rally cars were much closer to the specifications of the real world road cars.

Ralliart Europe's first driver was Finland's Lasse Lampi, who began his work for the team by driving a Starion Turbo. Since then many illustrious names have followed Lampi behind the wheel of various Mitsubishis for Ralliart Europe. The list includes – in alphabetical order, nothing more – Pentti Arikkala, Richard Burns, François Delecour, Kenneth Eriksson, Freddy Loix, Tommi Makinen, Alister McRae, Timo Salonen, Armin Schwarz, and Ari Vatanen. Since those early days of the Mitsubishi Starion Turbo, the team has competed with variants of the Galant VR-4 and, more importantly for us, the Lancer Evolution.

The wisdom of putting together a UK-based team to compete on the European circuit began to pay off quickly with wins in the Galant on the 1000 Lakes as well as the RAC Rally in 1989. Mitsubishi Ralliart Europe's influence was not always confined to its original remit, as was shown when the team triumphed in the 1987 Middle East Championship with the two-wheel-drive Starion Turbo, driven by Lampi.

By 1990 its Maldon base had become too small for the expanding Ralliart Europe team, so they made plans to move to larger premises in the heart of the UK's automotive industry. This would mean they had excellent engineering, technical, and design facilities close to hand, and the best talents the industry had to offer would be on their doorstep. The move was therefore made to Rugby in the West Midlands, where the company is still to be found today.

The FIA changed the rules of participation in the World Rally Championship for the 1995 season, making competing in each round compulsory. This meant the teams could no longer cherry-pick their favourite events, but had to field a team at each venue. Far from being a problem to Ralliart Europe, the compulsory participation has seen it move on to greater victories. Mitsubishi Ralliart Europe is the only World Rally Championship team to have won four consecutive Drivers' Championship titles, from 1996 to 1999. In 1998 the team also took the manufacturers' title.

Achieving so much in just a few years has shown that Ralliart Europe is a useful asset to a company like Mitsubishi. Even in the modern business world where costs are being slashed at every opportunity, Mitsubishi has emphatically declared an ongoing commitment to motorsport. And, although at the time of writing Mitsubishi had pulled out of competition to further develop the new Lancer Evolution WRC, Ralliart Europe will be back to contest the 2004 season of the World Rally Championship.

obviously working for Loix, as he improved to fourth. The grippy tarmac was better suited to his driving style than the slippery rough stuff.

Although neither driver could get to the top of the field in Australia, Makinen did manage a third place. More importantly his rival for the title, Auriol, retired early and scored nothing. This almost gave Tommi the title without going to the last event, but not quite.

At the RAC, Makinen again retired, but this time it was engine failure rather than mixing it with immovable lumps of scenery. But instead of going on to take the trophy for that year, Auriol also retired on the stage after. This meant that Makinen won the trophy again – a total of four consecutive wins of the World Rally Championship title.

Toyota had already won the manufacturers' title, but Mitsubishi's dismay at losing out in the manufacturer series was more than covered by Tommi's amazing feat. To celebrate the fact that Makinen was on top of the pile again, Mitsubishi decided to do something special to commemorate it. That something special was the Mitsubishi Evo VI Tommi Makinen Edition.

Back in the APRC the winning bug had bitten Mitsubishi again, and it had a one–two with Katsuhiko Taguchi taking top spot ahead of last year's runner-up, Kataoka.

2000

Although it was obvious that a WRC car could be modified far in excess of Group A, Mitsubishi didn't want to change the habits that had led them to be so successful over the previous seasons. Although they were more closely hemmed in by the regs, a process of constant development meant Evos could almost change spec with every round of the championship – particularly when so much of the engine and transmission performance was computer controlled. Tweaks could be performed on a laptop and the drivers could feel the results immediately.

The year started on a very positive note for Tommi Makinen when he won the Monte Carlo Rally after going ahead on the fourth stage and then disappearing off in to the distance. Freddy Loix wasn't quite as happy, though, never really getting on the pace and finally finishing in sixth position. He suffered similar maladies on the next event in Sweden where he dropped down to eighth place, coming home well behind Makinen, who was knocked into second place by Marcus Gronholm.

Things didn't get any better on the Safari Rally either. Both Makinen and Loix retired from the event – Tommi with electrical *and* suspension problems, and Freddy with just one helping of suspension trouble. A reversal of fortune didn't appear for Makinen on the Portuguese Rally either, and his car went out after a crash damaged the suspension beyond use. Loix managed to get home and rescue some points for Mitsubishi's manufacturer challenge, but his sixth place didn't fill the coffers much.

The Spanish event gave Makinen something to be pleased about because he managed to finish fourth even though his car was afflicted with transmission problems. Loix also made it to the end of the rally, but was some

DID YOU KNOW?

Not only was Alister McRae following in the wheel tracks of his older brother Colin – who had been the first British World Rally Champion for years when he took the title in 1995 – but they were both following their father Jimmy, who had been five times British Champion. Definitely something in the genes, then. Colin was the youngest-ever champ, taking the world title when he was just 27.

way down in eighth place. Argentina was slightly better for Makinen when he managed to move up to a third-place finish, while Loix took advantage of a lot of retirements to come in fifth. Unfortunately it wasn't a turn of fortune for the Mitsubishi team, as Greece would prove.

On the Acropolis Rally both Makinen and Loix went out on the first stage following breakdowns. This run of awful luck followed them all the way to New Zealand, where they both failed to finish again. Makinen had a crash which was put down to diff troubles, and Loix retired. It was a lacklustre end to the Evo VI's rally career, but the revamped Evo VI½ was waiting to bring the team better results, starting on the Finn's home rally.

Again it was a case of poor luck and persistence, with Loix retiring with an overheated engine after puncturing the car's radiator during a small off. The persistence came from Makinen, who was struggling with the new car's suspension but still managed to finish fourth. At the Cyprus Rally Makinen's Evo suffered from transmission troubles that held him back even though he was driving brilliantly. His fifth place was three better than Loix's eighth, but at least Mitsubishi had two cars finishing the event.

It was a short respite though, because the Tour de Corse event saw both cars crash out. With his failure to finish, Makinen effectively saw his chances of a fifth drivers' title disappear. Maybe that knocked some of the wind out of his sails because he performed somewhat below par on the San Remo event that followed, finally coming in third. Loix got his car to the finish in eighth place again, the fourth time he'd done it that season.

As what must have seemed a final insult in a poor season, Mitsubishi was ruled to have been using an illegal turbocharger on the Australian Rally, so Makinen was excluded from the results, losing a fine comeback victory. The odd thing was that the infringement was a matter of interpretation, and Mitsubishi hadn't actually been cheating, as Toyota had done a few years previously. The 'illegal' turbo offered no performance advantage and, because he was right behind Makinen in second place, Marcus Gronholm would have won the drivers' title anyway.

The final event of the year was again the RAC Rally, and Loix's run of poor luck capped the season with him rolling off the course on the second stage. Makinen did get his car to the end of the rally, but even pushing to the limit he could only manage third. The season ended with him in fifth place in the drivers' standings, while Mitsubishi had dropped to fourth in their title chase. It seemed to be finally hitting home that the WRC advantage was one that was going to be too big to get over with a Group A car, so Mitsubishi had to consider carefully what to do for the coming season.

2001

It seemed that the only course of action left for Mitsubishi in 2001 was to bite the bullet and build a WRC car like everyone else. Then they could join the other manufacturers in a rally series made up of cars that looked vaguely like their street-bound counterparts but were very different under the skin. Instead, Mitsubishi arrived for the first event with the Evo VI½ and the same driver teams that they'd had throughout the previous year.

Behind the scenes, work was going on to turn the a new Cedia-based car into an Evolution to carry on the famous name. This would then form the basis for a WRC monster that could fight it out with the new front-runners who were pushing the WRC regs as hard as possible.

Unfortunately, Mitsubishi didn't have the right car to turn into a WRC contender until the Cedia-based Evo VII was announced the week after the Monte Carlo Rally. Then it would take another six months before Ralliart made an announcement of their own to say that the Evo VII WRC car would make its debut on the San Remo Rally in October 2001.

To a lot of people it seemed strange to launch such a radical car so far into a season, but there was a very good reason behind it. Mitsubishi had an agreement with the FIA that a Mitsubishi WRC car would begin competing at the earliest possible opportunity in return for them being allowed to compete with the Group A cars until then. Bearing in mind when the Evo VII was launched, it would have been difficult for Mitsubishi to hold on to the WRC version until the beginning of the 2002 season.

With a freer hand to modify the base vehicle to WRC standards, Mitsubishi majored on three areas of the Cedia to get the Evo version working well. To begin with there was a much wider range of mods allowed to the suspension set-up, so the whole of the Mitsubishi's rear end was swapped over to a MacPherson strut system similar to the front end. There was also greater suspension travel to improve traction on the really rough stuff, and the longer wheelbase of the Cedia helped with stability at high speed. The wheel arches were also pulled to give more clearance for the larger wheels and greater travel.

In an effort to improve the car's weight distribution the motor was shifted back in the engine bay by 25mm (1in). It might not sound a lot, but moving that amount of weight has a noticeable effect on the way a car handles, so it was worth doing for this level of competition. An added bonus of shifting the lump was that tyre wear improved.

The engine also came in for more work, but it was all based around lightening components and reducing friction, both of which helped to get the motor to spin up faster and get on boost earlier. While the responsiveness of the engine was markedly improved, the power and torque figures were only up by a little. Still, it's not how much you've got, it's how you use it, isn't it?

As it turned out, Makinen was back to his winning ways from the off, taking the Monte Carlo with little trouble. And someone must have given Loix a motivational pep talk, because he even managed to set a fastest time on one of the stages. He couldn't repeat this across the event, though, and finished in sixth place. Maybe Mitsubishi didn't need to rush that Evo VII along after all.

Or maybe they did. The second rally of the year wasn't so successful for Makinen when he crashed out of the runner-up spot on the final day. Loix had been rambling in his car twice, but still managed to get back on track to finally come in 13th. Happily for Mitsubishi, Thomas Radstrom was also tooling round in a Mitsubishi Carisma GT – essentially a rebadged Lancer Evo, and what Loix had been driving for the past two seasons – and he finished in second.

The rally in Portugal proved to be a wet and muddy affair, but it didn't matter to Tommi as he was back on top regardless of the weather, though Loix retired with clutch problems while holding fifth place. Makinen's points helped him and Mitsubishi to the top of both the drivers' and manufacturers' tables.

The fourth outing of the year at the Spanish round of the WRC was hampered by a lack of grip for the Mitsubishi drivers, but they still managed to get third and fourth places, with Makinen showing the young Belgian the way home again. In Argentina Makinen slipped to fourth place in the rally and was beginning to be reeled in by the guy who was second in the Drivers' Championship, Carlos Sainz. Mitsubishi were also being closed down by Ford, who were just eight points behind.

The Cyprus Rally was to further hinder the chances of Makinen and Mitsubishi when he went off the stage on the first day. Freddy did manage fifth place, but Colin McRae's win had put Ford ahead, while Tommi was only one point in front in the drivers' league.

The Acropolis dented Makinen's title chances further when he ended up with a fourth-place finish and sharing the Drivers' Championship lead with McRae.

DID YOU KNOW?

While everyone was getting excited about the road car running with four-pot Brembo brakes, the Evo WRC used water-cooled eight-pot calipers on high-speed tarmac events. Now we haven't seen any of those on a road-going version yet...

Loix had more problems when his gearbox played up and the intercooler was damaged. He did manage to get the car home though, just squeaking in to the top ten with ninth place.

Just when Tommi really needed some good karma on the Safari Rally, it arrived two-fold. Not only did he win the event easily – some 12 minutes ahead of his nearest, Peugeot-mounted rival – but Colin McRae didn't complete the course. This put Makinen ten points clear of McRae, and Mitsubishi six points ahead of Ford. Freddy Loix also had a little helping hand after some engine trouble threatened to end his rally. A swift cylinder head change got him going well enough to allow him to finish in fifth place – probably a lot better than he'd thought he would do. But one reasonable rally doesn't make a season, and the next event saw more trials and tribulations.

On his return to the 1000 Lakes in Finland, Makinen retired on the first stage after damaging his car during a crash. Loix at least made it through the event, but his tenth place didn't help Mitsubishi's championship endeavours. Hopefully the New Zealand Rally would be a fitting end to the Evo VI½'s career.

Sadly the old car went out with a whimper rather than a bang. Makinen finished ahead of Loix, as he'd almost always done, but eighth and 11th weren't going to make any inroads into McRae's or Ford's challenges. Makinen and McRae were level after New Zealand, but Ford were ten points ahead of Mitsubishi.

San Remo was the debut of the Lancer Evolution WRC, but it started with the same ill fortune as the Evo VI½ had ended. Makinen was lying 11th, well off the pace, when he crashed and lost a wheel. Again Loix managed to get his car home, but he only finished in 12th spot. It was a very different opening to an Evo's campaign than those enjoyed by any of the previous variants. Surely things couldn't get any worse?

Well, actually, they could. And they did. On the Tour de Corse Makinen crashed out so heavily that his co-driver Risto Mannisenmaki was badly injured and had to miss the remaining rounds of the season. And Loix had a couple of early punctures which cost him lots of

Although he was a master on the Scandinavian snow, Makinen and his Evo VI went out of the 2001 Swedish Rally while lying in second place. (Ralliart Europe)

time. So much time that at one point he was lying in 73rd place. He did manage to claw a lot of it back, but even so he only finished in 12th. The only good thing to come out of the Corsican event was that McRae also didn't score any points, so he and Makinen were still tied for the championship lead.

For the Australian event Makinen was partnered by Timo Hautunen, and the new pairing managed to improve the Evolution WRC's rally record by getting it home in sixth place. The only slight problem was that McRae finished one place higher than Tommi, and so went one point into the lead in the drivers' league. Loix was hampered by electrical problems that kept him down in 11th position, and Mitsubishi's chances of doing anything in the Manufacturers' Championship were long gone.

Although Makinen had never done particularly well on the RAC Rally, he was mildly hopeful because of the way the Evo WRC was improving all the time. And he needed every bit of good fortune to win his fifth title. Going into the RAC there were four drivers who could win the championship given the right circumstances, so there was fierce competition for the win. Makinen, McRae, Sainz, and Burns were all within striking distance of the title.

Another battle surrounded Makinen, Juha Kankkunen, Carlos Sainz, and Colin McRae. They all had 23 wins each, so whichever of the four won next would be WRC's most successful driver ever. It wasn't destined to be Makinen, as he crashed out of the RAC very early on, which was a sad way to end his association with Mitsubishi after so many years of competitive and successful rallying. Freddy Loix's season also finished on a bum note when he went out with transmission problems. Of the four-way fight for WRC honours, Burns was the victor, even though he'd only won one event during the year, and both McRae and Makinen had won three each.

2002

The new season saw new faces in the Mitsubishi camp, with François Delecour and Alister McRae doing the driving and Daniel Grataloup and David Senior telling them where to go – so to speak. Delecour had been driving successfully for years while Alister McRae came from a rallying family that had won plenty of trophies.

Unfortunately, no-one had told the WRC scriptwriters that Mitsubishi's men should be at the front. The season started poorly and then got worse. With Delecour coming home in ninth place, and McRae managing to

limp home to 14th after gouging a chunk out of a wall, the Monte Carlo proved a tough debut for the new boys. What the rest of the team thought of Tommi Makinen's eventual victory in a Subaru isn't recorded, but the irony must have been there for all to see.

Moving to Sweden didn't help the team much, as Delecour had an excursion into a ditch that dropped him well down the field and new boy Jani Paasonen lost a wheel after hitting a concealed rock. McRae did give the team some better news by getting home in eighth place, so maybe things were turning round.

The new position for the Tour de Corse in the calendar meant everyone was unsure of how the weather was going to affect the rallying, and the changeable conditions did catch a few people out. Both Mitsubishi men suffered when rain hit the event, but still managed to finish the rally in seventh and tenth places, with Delecour scoring points for Mitsubishi's manufacturers' league position but just missing out on some for his personal tally.

Things didn't improve much in the Spanish Rally that followed, and in fact it was the last event that season where both cars managed to finish together. Even when Paasonen bolstered the team to three runners, only one of them crossed the finish line each time. To add further insult to injury, the best position that a WRC Evo managed in the remaining events was eighth place, and at the end of 2002 Mitsubishi declared that it was pulling out of the championship so that it could spend a year sorting out a new entrant for an attack on the 2004 season.

This might seem like a strange move to some people, but taking the car out of the spotlight and doing some serious development work away from the glare of publicity that surrounds every WRC event has to be a good idea. There can be little doubt that the engineering team will find out what the WRC Evo needs to get it back on fighting terms with the opposition, and that they'll get that done for the Monte Carlo Rally in 2004. It'll be good to see an Evo back at the front of WRC after so long.

Goings on in Group N

While everyone was avidly watching the Group A battles at the head of the field, the Group N contestants were getting on with their racing and often finishing in the overall top ten – and ahead of the faster cars from the higher class. During 1994 Isolde Holderied and Tina Thorner only just missed out on Group N honours after Holderied picked up the ladies' drivers' title. She

retained this title the year after, but another Evo driver, Rui Madeira, took the Group N title to complete a Mitsubishi double.

Although Holderied wasn't in a Mitsubishi in 1996, Tina Thorner had moved over to co-drive Uwe Nittel's Evo in Group N, and they were runners-up in the championship that year. Another Lancer driver, Gustavo Trelles, won the title, so at least Mitsubishi retained the individual award. Trelles obviously had a liking for the Group N championship because he was back in 1997. He retained the title with the astonishing feat of scoring three times the number of points of his nearest rival. Although he didn't get quite as far ahead in 1998, he still managed to hold on to his crown for a third consecutive time, keeping station with Tommi Makinen over in Group A.

Alister McRae shows off the Evolution WRC to rally fans at the Rally Supercar day at Castle Combe, 2002. Mitsubishi didn't contest the 2003 WRC championship, but they plan to return in 2004 to try and recapture the success of the late 1990s. (Ralliart Europe)

This status quo was to continue in 1999, when Trelles again cleaned up in Group N. In some events he did better than the Group A combinations that should have been miles ahead. Unfortunately, Trelles couldn't continue his run of good fortune in Group N forever, and the 2000 season was the one where he dipped out at the end. Still, he did manage to come home second in the championship. The eventual winner was Manfred Stohl, who was driving another Lancer Evolution.

Chapter Seven

You pays your money...

Once you've decided to take the plunge and buy a piece of motoring history like an Evo, you'll have to decide which version you're going to go for. From a monetary point of view, the earlier cars are obviously cheaper, but there are generally less of them to choose from because fewer have been exported outside Japan than the later models. I should know. Finding early cars to photograph was a bit like *Mission: Impossible...*

Having decided which version is going to be best for you, the job of tracking down a good one starts. Actually finding the right car is something that might take months, but if you begin by looking in the right places, it could be a lot quicker. Being a very special car they don't often turn up in the local free newspaper, so one of the best places to start chasing one down is through the owners' club website. This should let you see a few examples of the one you're after, and you can always post a request for what you want if you can't find it straight away. Who knows, someone who was considering selling their car might be spurred into action if someone else is actively searching for what they've got.

Also, when you look at club cars you'll probably be buying something that's been owned and looked after by an enthusiast. This can be a bit of a double-edged sword if the enthusiast was keen on using his or her Evo on track days at every available opportunity, but it should mean that it's been well cared for by someone who thinks of it as more than just A-to-B transport. And anyway, once you've read this chapter, the signs of 'enthusiastic' use will be obvious.

Another advantage of buying a car from its owner rather than a garage forecourt is that you can get a sense of how the seller feels about their Mitsi, and what reasons have brought it onto the market. If they've only had the car for a few months, why are they getting rid of

it so quickly? While they might have a very genuine reason for the sale, you could get an inkling that it hasn't been a good purchase and they're now trying to off-load their problem onto someone else. On the other hand, if they've had the car for a couple of years, and they're actively looking for a newer replacement or there's another Evo on the drive already, you're probably onto a fairly safe bet.

Of course, you could check out some cars at an importer's showroom. You'll probably find a large selection of Evos to look at if you search the internet and trawl through the garage websites, and you'll be able to discount the ones that don't look like they fit the bill before you waste any fuel or time going for a look. Being the first person to own the car in this country can be a bit of a gamble, but if you've got a decent warranty, and you inspect the car thoroughly enough, you should be OK.

When you start looking over a prospective purchase, look really hard. What at first glance seems to be a pristine example might not be so good when you get up close. See how this paint is flaking away around the side repeater lamp? What history was covered up by the respray?

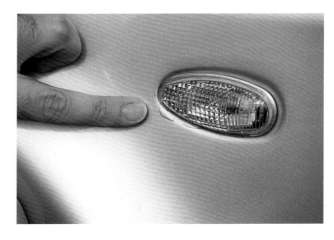

Left: A nasty chip on the edge of a panel could be sorted easily, but why is it there in the first place? If you find any imperfections in the body condition, ask some awkward questions.

Below left: Wheel arches come in for some rough treatment from tyre debris, and it's easy for them to be damaged to the point where rust sets in. Be careful you don't miss the signs that the tin worm is in residence.

Another showroom option is the performance car specialist, who'll have not only Evos but anything sporty littering the place. There are plenty of these garages around now, but you'll have to make sure you're really happy with the people who run the place before you think of handing over any money. Some have been known to open and close very quickly and, if they go pop soon after you've bought your car, you'll have no comeback over any mechanical problems later.

So, once you've found a prospective Evo to check out – and you've evaluated the vendor and feel sure that they aren't just trying to hang an impressive but expensive millstone around your neck – what should you look at on the car itself? Obviously, there are plenty of model-specific items that need checking out, but there are quite a few general things to look at, regardless of which Evo you're considering. We'll deal with these first.

Mechanically, the Mitsubishi doesn't have too many areas that are known trouble-spots. Most of the mechanical problems that occur are down to insufficient or incorrect maintenance, so that's another good reason to get an idea of how well the car has been looked after in the past few years, if that's at all possible. This is where you could hit a problem with an imported early model because, unless you're very lucky, it will come with no service history documents. If the car does have some paperwork with it, you've got precious little chance of understanding what it all means, but at least it's nice to have a few stamps in a service book. If there's nothing, you'll have to be even more careful.

If you are a bit unsure about the mechanical ins and outs of buying a second-hand car, you should definitely try and get an Evo-owning friend, or someone who can give an unbiased opinion on the vehicle's condition and value for money, to accompany you. If all else fails, there are plenty of companies like the AA or RAC who offer to come and examine a car, and give a full written report that goes into some depth. Obviously, this service is an added cost, but if it means you know all about the

When you find evidence of a respray like this bad masking around the door handle (above) or the overspray on the black panel (below), you need to find out how bad the damage was that prompted the repair.

Low spoilers are always going to be prone to scratches and scuffs, but just make sure that's all it is and not a pointer to some other problem that could be expensive to sort out.

problems before you either buy the car or walk away from it, it will be money well spent. Just be aware that the assessor a big national company could send might not have had many dealings with something as specialised as an Evo. It's up to you to make sure that whoever you choose has people well versed in high performance cars.

If you decide to have a go yourself – and plenty of people do – a careful walk-round is a good way to start an appraisal. During this you should look at how the panels fit, and at the general condition of the paintwork. Bodged repairs are normally easy to pick up, and you should be able to look down the sides of the car to see how straight or rippled it is. Don't forget that the aluminium bonnet – and wings on Evo Vs onwards – can be easily dinged, so check them carefully for signs of damage that needs sorting, or badly bodged repairs.

You can also see if the previous owner used a sponge and leather to wash their pride and joy, or whether it was regularly scoured in a car wash. The latter method of cleaning takes a big toll on the car's finish and can ruin paintwork to the point of needing remedial surgery at a bodyshop. In less severe cases a can of cutting compound and a weekend spent carefully removing the dead and scuffed top layer of paint will achieve a real turnaround in the finish. But if the seller hasn't done this to spruce the car up a bit and make it look more desirable, you have to ask yourself how well they've looked after it for the rest of the time they've owned it.

During your examination of the car's outside condition, you should also look at the wheels. Almost all the cars you'll see – unless it's an incredibly original RS model, and there aren't many of those around – will be on alloy rims, which can be easily damaged by careless driving. If the rims aren't obviously kerbed and buckled, they should be serviceable enough, but just check that they haven't been bulled up to hide more major defects. If they're a bit scuffed and peeling, look a lot closer. Heavily kerbed rims, ingrained brake dust, and flaky lacquer can normally be repaired by an alloy wheel refurbishing specialist, but getting it done properly isn't a cheap job. In the worst cases the wheels could be so far gone that they'll need replacing rather than

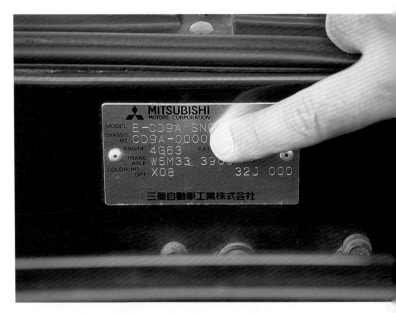

Although it is easily moved from one car to another, the VIN plate should tally with the car. Make sure all the numbers are the same between car and logbook.

repairing, and that's obviously a very expensive option. And, given the complexities of the Evo's suspension, any dings on the wheel could also have upset the critical suspension geometry.

While you're grubbing round on the floor, have a quick look at the tyres. They should look properly inflated and have even wear across the tread. Any bald lines can show that something is amiss with the suspension settings, or that the owner is running the tyres at totally the wrong pressure, but either way it's a warning sign. If there are brand new tyres on the car, just ask why they've put new rubber on. They might have just saved you some money, or they might be trying to hide some expensive repairs that you could end up paying for in the long run.

And while you're giving the wheels a once-over, have a good look through them at the brakes, particularly on anything that has the big shiny Brembo four-pot calipers. On the earlier cars fitted with non-Brembo brakes you're looking for the general condition of the calipers and disc rotors. If the car has only just come into the country you might find that the discs are very corroded and just about fit for scrap. If they're nice and smooth under a light coating of surface rust you'll probably get away with it and just rub off the oxidisation by driving around for a while. However, if the disc is heavily grooved and rusty, you've got a great bargaining chip. Evolution discs aren't cheap items, so make sure the cost of swapping them is taken into consideration. If after-market drilled discs have been fitted, look for cracking.

Check the calipers aren't badly corroded either. The trip from Japan on the boat can take its toll on the braking system, so if you're going to be the first UK

DID YOU KNOW?

If you're considering buying from a private seller there are a couple of extra things to consider. Try and make sure the driveway the car's parked in does actually belong to the vendor, and you're not about to become the victim of a scam. Remember that if the car turns out to be stolen it will be confiscated and you'll have lost both your money and your new motor.

With the earlier Evolutions being grey imports, someone will have had to fit a fog light to make them legal on UK roads. Just hope that it wasn't done in an afterthought way like this.

Top left: That's better. Someone has taken the time to cut the fog light neatly into the rear bumper, where it looks better and is less prone to accidental damage.

Top right: It might only look like a minor scuff, but it could be a sign that there's more damage hidden from view; and it could also cost a decent chunk to get it fixed properly.

Left: Missing covers like these often mean someone's been behind the scenes, and not cared too much about putting things right once they've finished. If something looks wrong, find out what happened before you start exchanging cash.

owner you need to be sure that everything's in good nick, otherwise you've got a nice fat bill on the way almost before you've started.

On Brembo-equipped cars you should also take note of the colour of the calipers, as well as the disc condition. These calipers were painted bright red with a brilliant white 'Brembo' logo stencilled onto the outside. What you should be looking for is the actual colour of the caliper, to give an indication of how hard the brakes have been used. If the car has done regular motoring, the calipers should still be pristine red and white, even if you have to wipe away a bit of brake dust to be able to tell. If the Evo has spent plenty of time on the track being used hard, the paint changes colour. If the caliper appears to be a dull slightly browny-red, and the logo looks like it's gone a bit yellowed, the calipers have seen some serious work and been cooked. Once you've worked that out, you can quiz the owner on how many track sessions they do. If they come clean, no problem. If they reckon they never go near a circuit, they're either telling porkies, or they

Import cars often lack history and sometimes they don't come with vital pieces of equipment. This CD player requires a remote control to use it, which was missing from the car. At least the Japanese owner had fitted a rear strut brace.

drive incredibly hard on the open road. Either way you might want to be a bit more wary of the car and the vendor.

After you've inspected the exterior, the next port of call should be the engine bay. The most obvious thing to check is the overall cleanliness of the motor and the surrounding panelwork. If everything is in a uniform state, and maybe a little dirty, this is normally a good sign. It should mean there have been no serious body repairs, and that the mechanicals are reliable enough not to need constant attention.

If, on the other hand, one inner wing panel is pristine while the other one is filthy, you have to ask why. Does it mean that one side of the car has been attended to after an accident? If you do spot this, start digging further. Are there any new hose clips holding pipes in place? Do any of the pipes look like they've been changed recently? Is one section of wiring loom much newer than the rest, and are the standard wiring clips intact or have they been replaced with cable ties? Is there evidence of overspray tucked away in difficult-to-reach corners?

You're also looking for evidence of old repairs, so check the weld seams around the strut towers and the condition of the chassis legs down the side of the engine while you're under there. Any rust trails on the welds, or kinks and rust spots on the legs, could point to damage received some time in the past that's beginning to show through now.

If, after you've checked round, you get the feeling that the car has been repaired, ask some polite but awkward questions about its history. If you don't like the answers you get, walk away and look elsewhere. If the seller allays your fears, it could be worth carrying on with the examination. Being built for rallying means that Evos are pretty robust vehicles, so a little bit of a crunch isn't the end of the world. That is, as long as the vendor has adjusted the sale price to suit the car's imperfect history, and he or she is happy to tell you the extent of the damage. You could still get a solid car, and use the money you save on the purchase price to add to

The more supportive Recaros fitted in Evo IIs can often suffer from collapsed side bolsters, like this one, which shows where the driver gets in and out of the seat.

the modification budget. (Let's face it, there *is* going to be a modification budget, isn't there?)

Assuming you're happy with the bits you've looked at on the outside and under the front, it's the turn of the interior to be scrutinised. Telltale signs of heavy wear on the steering wheel rim, seat bolsters, pedal rubbers, gear lever, and handbrake can all let you know that the car has covered a serious amount of miles, so check what you're seeing against the odometer reading. Evo interior bits aren't cheap or plentiful (you'll see this is a recurring theme with just about all Evo stuff...) so replacing Recaro seats or trim work isn't something you want to be contemplating unless the car is very cheap.

If the mileage appears to be low for the car's age, ask for some proof to back up the figures. You have to keep remembering that the Evolution is a high-performance sports car masquerading as a family saloon, so a lot of them will have been used for pleasure rather than as day-to-day hacks. Don't be too suspicious if the mileage only went up a few thousand between MOTs, especially if there are other family runabouts on the drive that could have been the regular daily driver.

Another thing to check when you're in the boot is the steel floor under the carpet. Apart from a few obvious moulding lines, the floor should be flat. If there are any non-standard ripples in it, the chances are that the car has been heavily thumped and then pulled straight, so you might want to walk away. The boot should also be nice and dry under the carpet, and the space-saver spare and jack should be present and in good nick. If there's no boot trim the car is probably an RS, so make sure that's what you're supposed to be buying.

If you're still happy with the car, you should get the keys and start the motor. Look for oily smoke coming from the exhaust instead of healthy-looking steam, but be aware that Evos do tend to run a bit rich on cold start, so a smoky exhaust isn't necessarily indicative of a problem if the motor is cold. Check again when everything is warmed up, and see if the smoke has gone then. If there are still oily wisps coming out, the turbo or the engine could need some major work. And that won't be cheap.

One service item that needs textbook attention is the cambelt. The cost of swapping a cambelt is far lower than the cost of putting right the damage that occurs when it snaps. If you can get a peep at the cambelt – unlikely, but we live in hope – and it looks shiny and possibly even a bit grooved on the outside, you need documented proof that it has been changed in the last

You can see radial cracks like these without removing a wheel, so look hard for them if the Evo you're inspecting has drilled discs. Either get the price down to cover new ones, or get them changed before you part with your cash.

25,000 miles (40,000km), or you need to budget on doing it as soon as you get it home. If you are planning to have your new car thoroughly serviced once you've bought it – which isn't a bad idea anyway – it might be as well to do the belt while you're there.

Take the opportunity to check all the electrical functions to make sure they perform as they should, and note anything that appears to have stopped working. Evos don't really have any electrical woes as a breed, but individual cars could have failures that still need sorting. In general, you have to be aware that electrical faults can be time-consuming and costly things to trace and cure, but that they can also be good bargaining tools to help you reduce the asking price if you're prepared to have a go at finding the problem, or you have a tame electrical specialist who can give you a hand. Check particularly things like the intercooler water spray, which generally isn't an often-used item, just to make sure everything's still in working order.

The test drive should be used as the final check that the car is still worth buying. There should be no sloppiness in the brakes, the steering should be positive and without any discernible play, and the engine and gearbox should perform without any tantrums. There are also particular things to check on the different models, but we'll come to those in a minute.

If the car seems to creak and rattle all the time, this could be a sign that it's had a hard life thumping across

This caliper used to be bright red and have white writing. Do you reckon the owner might have been using the brakes enthusiastically round a track? I think he probably has...

the rumble strips while someone was playing out their racing driver fantasies. Obviously, if it's an early car then there are going to be more squeaks and groans simply because of its age and mileage, but if the Evo feels very loose and flimsy, you might want to try another one or two before you finally get out your chequebook.

Not only should the car feel nice and tight, but it should perform well. Even an Evo I has 250bhp, so unless you've turned up for the test drive in something similarly powerful you should be impressed. If everything appears in order, but you don't get pushed back in to the seat when you give it a bootful, there's obviously something wrong. If at all possible it would be worth trying to get behind the wheel of a well-sorted Evo before you start your quest, and then you'll have some sort of benchmark as to how your prospective purchase is performing.

One final point is that you shouldn't dismiss non-standard cars that have been tweaked a bit. The chances are that once you've had your Evo for a while you'll want a bit more power, so if you can find a car that's already had a few mods done, it could save you money in the long run. Just make sure you aren't paying a hefty premium for the additional bits, otherwise you might as well buy a standard car and then do the tweaks your-self. Also, if the car has a cat-bypass pipe fitted, make sure the owner has the original cat before you do the deal. If they haven't got the pipe, you'll have to buy one to get the car through its MOT, and that won't be cheap.

So, having gone over a few general things, let's get specific. We'll start with the Evo I–III, and then major on the IV–VI. Because the VII hasn't been out as long there isn't really a lot to check out other than the possibility of accident damage and a few foibles that it inherited from the VI, but these are mentioned where appropriate. And no, I'm not mentioning the VIII, because as I wrote this Mitsubishi had only just admitted it was going to be coming to the UK at all. By the time this book comes out the Evo VIII will have been on sale for only a few months.

Evolution I–III

The thing to remember about Evos I–III is that there are a lot fewer of them about in the UK than the later models, so you have to check carefully that the car you are examining is actually an Evo of the type described, or, in some cases, an Evo at all. With the body addenda being bolt-on items, it's possible to make an Evo I look like a III, and even to turn an ordinary Lancer GSR – or even a Proton – into a fake Evo.

The problems come about from two separate areas. Firstly, there's a Lancer GSR powered by a turbo 1.8-litre motor and fitted with a four-wheel-drive system. After whacking on a few external goodies, an ordinary GSR could pass for an Evo as long as someone wasn't looking too hard, and didn't have such a long-running list of what to check. The other car that can be turned into a poor Evo copy is a Proton Persona. The body looks almost identical to the real deal, and if there's a dead or stolen Evo to transplant bits from, the potential profit to be made from a few hours in the garage has turned some people's heads. So how do you spot a hooky Evo?

To find out if the car is actually fitted with a 2.0-litre turbo 4G63 motor you need to check three things. The 1.8-litre is quite a bit smaller than the 2.0-litre, so if there seems to be a lot of space around the motor, that could be one giveaway. If you're unsure about how big the real Evo engine should be, you've still got two more clues to check. Firstly, there's the oil filler cap position.

DID YOU KNOW?

Isn't the internet a wonderful thing? For a small fee you can now check out any prospective vehicle on the web, and it's well worth finding out if the car you're thinking of shelling out coin for has outstanding finance, or has ever been on the insurance register.

On a 4G63 lump this is fitted at the cambelt-cover end of the engine, over the inlet cam, so it's nearer the back of the engine bay. The 1.8-litre oil filler is at the same end of the motor, but it fits in over the exhaust cam, so it's nearer the front of the car.

The final check is to look where the radiator top-hose comes out of the cylinder head at the opposite end to the cambelt. If the outlet is on the front of the motor, you can bet the oil filler is also at the front, because this is the 1.8-litre car and congratulations, you've just caught a forgery. Make your excuses and leave now! If, however, the water outlet is on the end of the head, the oil filler will be at the back of the cam cover, and you're looking at a real 4G63 motor.

Using the photographs in the earlier chapter on the first Evos, you should be able to make sure the car is exactly what the seller is claiming it is. To quickly sum up what extras each car should be wearing, we'll start with the Evo I. This has a vented bonnet, a bumper with no bottom lip, no sideskirts, and a hoop spoiler with a single centre support bar. This is bolted straight to the boot lid with no wicker underneath it. Finally, there are reflectors on either side of the rear number plate instead of fog lights.

The Evo II has the same bonnet as the Evo I, and the same front bumper, but the II also has a rubber lip fitted along the bottom edge of the bumper. Again there are no sideskirts, but the rear spoiler is now fitted onto a wicker that also has 'Evolution II' moulded into the centre of the trailing edge. Fog lights may also have been fitted in place of the rear reflectors of the Evo I.

The Evo III is the most radical-looking of the bunch. The front bumper is much wider and more aggressive than the others, and it has a lower section with two widely-spaced brake-cooling vents, and a centre louvre with two horizontal slats. The front indicators should have orange lenses with clear bulbs, whereas the Evo I and II have clear lenses with orange bulbs. Sideskirts have also entered the picture and they are embossed with 'Evolution III'. The rear spoiler has now become a proper wing, with the high-level brake light built into the rear edge of the wicker rather than the blade.

Now comes the difficult bit. Any or all of these items could have been retrofitted from a later car to an earlier one, so we'd better have a look at some other clues. All three Evos were fitted with 15in wheels. The first ones had silver six-spoke Mitsubishi items, the later two had OZ Racing five-spoke rims. Of course, anyone could have swapped these for something else by now, but it's worth a chance. Of course, if you're looking at an incredibly original – and incredibly rare – Evolution RS it might have steel wheels. That's very doubtful bearing in mind that most of them went straight into competition, but you never know. There may be a couple left.

This brings us to another little pitfall: trying to sort out the GSRs from the RSs. Inside the car there are a couple of other clues to look for. Early GSRs had

After the long trip from Japan any car's brakes will be a bit worse for wear, so check them carefully to see if the surface rust will wear off, or if the discs need swapping before you go any further.

Damaged wheels are costly to repair and very expensive to replace. Be sure you know what costs are going to be incurred before you agree a price for the car.

Recaros that have small side and base bolsters, and separate head restraints. Both IIs and IIIs have much deeper bolsters with shoulder support, as well as integrated headrests and an upper harness slot. The RS version had a very plain interior and poor seating that was designed to be changed for real motorsport equipment before the first competitive outing.

The Momo steering wheel is the same on the first two GSR models, with a more modern design of Momo fitted to the Evo III. All RS variants had the same Momo as fitted to the Evo I and II GSR. Then there's the glass-mounted rear wiper. No RS had a rear wiper, so if it's there, you're looking at a GSR. But if there's no rear wiper and the seller insists it's a GSR, check for the dashboard switch. The rear screen might have been replaced at some point in the past, but the wiring and switch will probably still be there. Finally, you can check the climate control with its digital display in the centre of the dash. It would be a murderous job to retrofit this item, so if it's there you're almost 100 per cent sure to be examining a GSR.

Another couple of giveaways are found on the vehicle exterior, although they're fairly minor. GSR door mirrors are body colour, as are the door handles – RS items were black. A black panel surrounds the RS number plate instead of the reflectors or fog lights on the GSR. Finally, GSRs were fitted with electric aerials on the rear wing whereas the RS had a manual aerial fitted into the driver's door pillar.

The biggest giveaway, and most difficult to replicate, is the ABS. All GSRs were fitted with it, so look for the

Once the car is in the UK and has been de-restricted, you must have tyres with the correct speed rating to allow you to use the Evo's performance safely.

orange warning light on the dash, and the brake distribution valve block under the bonnet. If the ABS is missing, the car's an RS – end of story.

If you get a combination of any of these items, you should be suspicious, and expect you're looking at an RS that someone's messed with. It might not be this owner who's tried to do the swaps, so don't get too heavy handed, just make your excuses and leave. If they genuinely don't know they were diddled when they bought the car, do you want to be the one to tell them?

If your suspicions are aroused, you could try checking the car's chassis number. Obviously this isn't a dead cert to establishing any car's validity because a Vehicle Identification Number (VIN) plate is pretty easy to drill off a genuine car and then rivet onto a wrong 'un. The Evolution I GSR was known as a CD9A-SNGF, while the Evo I RS was a CD9A-SNDF. The Evo II GSR was a CE9A-SNGF, and the Evo II RS was a CE9A-SNDF, but chassis numbers only ran up to 0008500. The Evolution III carried the same CE9A code, but its chassis numbers started at 01000001. Again, GSR was known as SNGF and RS was SNDF.

So, having finally established that the car is really what it purports to be, what else should we be checking to make sure that it's actually a car we might want to take away in return for large chunks of cash?

As well as the outline checks we've already talked about, there are a few specific areas to look at on Evo I–IIIs. Have a look through the bumper vents and see what condition the chassis legs and bumper mounts are in. These would probably take the brunt of a frontal impact, so they will show up any bodged repairs and be very rusty if things weren't done properly.

The other area to look at is the centre of the roof, about three-quarters of the way towards the back of the car. This area is where the internal bracing is bonded to the outer skin. For some reason the bonding material holds moisture and the roof skin can rust through. If there's anything bubbling in a line at this point, be prepared to get it repaired quickly before it eats a big hole in the roof and your wallet.

On the inside you should check that the correct seats are in place and solidly mounted. There shouldn't be any rocking around, but they should slide freely on their runners. And be sure to check both seats, just in case. Also, if you're looking at a GSR, make sure the electric mirrors not only adjust properly, but they also fold flat towards the car. While on the subject of electrical items, check the water spray works by operating the switch on

On early cars the rocker covers can weep a little oil, and that's nothing to worry about. Try wiping away the oily goo and then seeing if it comes back when the engine's running. If oil pumps out you must find out why before you buy.

the centre console near the gear lever. The jets are located behind the front number plate.

The last external checks should be done on the suspension. Make sure the car is sitting level, or possibly a little lower at the front. There should be no difference in side-to-side levels. Try bouncing each corner of the car to make sure the dampers are still damping. If the car hardly moves at all – and remember those thin wings when you're bouncing on the car – either the damper is seized up or the car has adjustable suspension and it's been set too hard. Find out which it is, because both need sorting, and readjusting suspension is a lot cheaper than replacing it. If the Evo

With so much trick suspension available for Japanese cars you might find your prospective purchase has something like these multi-adjustable units fitted. Have a good drive in the car and make sure you can live with the harsh ride, or find out how to soften them off and then try them again if you can.

passes this test, you should move on to the anti-roll bars and check their mounting bushes. This isn't too bad a job at the back because you can grab hold of the anti-roll bar and give it a shake. The front is difficult to get to, but you should try to get hold of it if you can and see if there's any play in the bushes.

Although the Evo is a supercar, it's also very user-friendly, and all the controls should be easily weighted rather than need the strength of a power-lifter to operate. The clutch pedal should have a long stroke which is pretty easy to use, so if it has a short stroke or is very heavy, you know there's a problem somewhere. Most likely is that the clutch pedal bracket will have cracked and this will be flexing instead of the pedal moving correctly. If you can, get someone to pump the pedal while you look at the bulkhead from under the bonnet. If the firewall flexes a lot, you have to presume the bracket needs sorting. It isn't a bad repair to do, but unless you have a welding plant and know how to use it, you're going to have to get it looked at professionally.

Under the bonnet there are a couple of things that you must check, otherwise you could be in for big bills. Although a uniformly mucky engine bay is OK, lots of oil dripping over things is definitely not. A little weep from the cam cover isn't too big a problem, and is one that can be fixed with sealant or a new gasket. A big leak – the sort of thing that comes back immediately it's been wiped clean – needs further investigation before you hand over cash.

Because the Evo is the type of car that attracts a performance-orientated driver, it might have been modified and, if it's been done properly, that isn't necessarily a bad thing. It saves you having to do it, doesn't it? But be sure you're happy that the work has been carried out correctly and, if it was a specialist job – meaning a bit more involved than just swapping an air filter or fitting an exhaust – find out who did it and be sure that they know what they're doing. There are plenty of Evo 'specialists' who are just garages jumping on the bandwagon when they really don't know one end of an Evo from the other.

Other checks should include popping the oil cap to have a quick look at the cam lobes visible underneath to see if they're in nice smooth condition, with no grooves or scratches. Also check under the cap for any signs of emulsified oil/water mix, also known as 'mayonnaise'. Generally, this is a sign that the head gasket is failing, but if there are only a few flecks it could just be that the car has been standing for some

Evolution's suffer from a corrosion problem on the roof. If you can see evidence of rust coming through, get it treated as soon as possible.

DID YOU KNOW?

If you really can't find anything you like in the UK, some specialist car importers will offer to source exactly what you want directly from Japan. The only thing to be aware of is that you need an escape clause if the vehicle that finally arrives isn't quite what you were expecting.

time and there's a little condensation in the motor, which isn't life threatening provided you get the oil changed quickly.

Next, whip out the dipstick and wipe the oil off with your fingers. The lubricant should be clean and smooth, rather than feeling gritty and looking like sludge. Also quiz the owner on how often they have the oil changed. The answer should be every 3,000 miles (4,800km). The area around the plenum should also be looked over to see if there are any signs of damage or leaking fuel.

If the car has the standard airbox, you could try opening it to make sure there's a filter inside. The precision internals of a turbo don't like ingesting anything other than nice clean air, so running without a filter is a big no-no. If there's a performance filter, check its condition to make sure it's not in need of imminent replacement.

You should also inspect the power steering reservoir to ensure the fluid is at the correct level and in good condition. Have a look at the master cylinders for brake and clutch, too, and the pipework surrounding them to see that everything looks in good condition.

Finally, take the radiator cap off and look at the coolant level and check that there is no oil or rust contamination. The coolant should have a slight tinge of blue/green from the antifreeze in the system, which is fine. You can look into the overflow tank to do the same thing. If it looks sludgy, that could be from oil contamination, and that could easily mean big bills are on the way.

This last test must only be carried out on a car with a cold engine and, if the vendor has warmed the engine through before you arrived to view the car, you might be a little bit suspicious. This is because any untoward noises are often easier to hear when the motor is stone cold. If the engine is warm, try and look around everything else and wait for it to cool down again, otherwise you might miss out on some vital symptoms.

If you do get to start a cold engine you'll probably notice a tapping noise from the top end of the motor, and this is fairly normal. For some reason an Evo's tappets are a bit noisy, and they're almost all like that. If the noise quietens down as the engine warms up, there's no problem. If there are persistent rattles that don't go as the engine temperature rises, you might want to get it investigated further.

Before you set off for a quick blast, check a few things with the gearbox first. Depress the clutch and try to get all the gears in the 'box. If any are difficult to engage or crunch going in, the clutch might be on the way out, or that pedal bracket might be flexing too much to allow full clutch travel. And just make sure the engine noise doesn't get any quieter when the clutch pedal is pressed in. If it does, the clutch release bearing is worn and that's what is making the noise.

If you do get out in the car and everything seems up to scratch, congratulations! You've just found a decent Evo and should be doing a deal for one of the most fun vehicles you'll buy. If the car doesn't make you grin from ear to ear with its lively performance and exemplary handling, you're either looking at a bit of a duffer, or you're looking at totally the wrong car for you.

Evolution IV–VI

Moving on to the newer Evo IV–VI series, there are plenty of things to check over when trying to find your perfect motoring partner. But at least we haven't heard of anyone trying to pass off another model of Mitsubishi as a genuine later Evo, so that's one less thing to worry about.

One of the more expensive things to check is the Active Yaw Control and the rear diff, which have a problem associated with the AYC computer control. Mitsubishi says the problem affects the late Evo IV and the early V, but you should check all cars for this just in case. What you're looking for is that the AYC computer should have been changed under a Mitsubishi recall, and that the diff hasn't been damaged by being run with a dodgy computer earlier in its life. You can find out if the computer has been changed by contacting Mitsubishi and checking chassis numbers with them, or the owner might know something about the work and be able to put your mind at ease.

To see if the diff is in good health, drive slow 90° turns, left and right, and listen for any weird noises coming from the back end. If everything appears silent, you should be OK, but if you can hear the diff

On later Evos this pipe vents internal engine pressure into the air system. This oil mist can attract dirt particles and when these clump together and become big enough to drop into the airstream and fly into the turbocharger, you could have expensive problems. Take off the large turbo air-feed pipe to see how it looks inside, just to be safe.

making a noise, even if the computer has been changed, the diff is probably on its way out. If it breaks, you'll be looking at a sizeable bill for a replacement unit. On the other hand, if someone has just changed a diff, but didn't know about the computer swap that is also required, the new diff will be on borrowed time too.

Going through the rest of the transmission there shouldn't be any other problems. Unless the car has been abused heavily on the track, the four-wheel-drive system is plenty strong enough to look after itself.

Some Japanese imports come loaded with goodies like this anodised radiator panel (left), or this Ralliart air filter element (below). Try not to pay over the odds for the extras, though, even if you really want them.

During the test drive make sure the gears swap cleanly without any crunching that could indicate weakened and damaged synchros.

If the gears are a bit reluctant to swap easily when the 'box is cold, but they feel crunch-free, it might just be that someone has used oil that's too thick, or they haven't used semi-synthetic oil. If the gearchange improves once the car is warmed through, you know that one of the first jobs you should do when you get it home is swap the oil for the right stuff. Also bear in mind that if the car is used heavily on the track the transmission oils should be changed after each session.

For heavy-duty use, Evo IV front brakes are a bit weak, so swapping to later-spec Brembos – or better – is always a good idea. If this has been done you can check the condition of the braking system with the colour test mentioned earlier. Also, when you're out on the road you'll be able to tell if the discs are warped when you use the brakes and get a wobbling through the steering wheel and/or a pulsing through the pedal. Even high-performance brakes can be used hard enough to warp them, particularly if the car does get track use.

Later Evos should also be subjected to the damper test, as they can begin to get tired by 40,000 miles (65,000km), and can start knocking as you drive. Bounce gently on the wing to see if the suspension deflects and then comes back to rest smoothly and quickly, without wobbling on, graunching, or being rock solid.

The rest of the car should be covered by the things we've already mentioned in the general section, but don't think that because the car is newer than an Evo I or III you can get away with looking less closely. Cars can be used and abused as soon as they hit the road, so go round any prospective purchase with a fine-tooth comb.

And if you really, *really* want an Evo, try to make sure the person going with you isn't totally convinced about you having one. That way they'll be more willing to point out any small defects that your rosy specs might want to look past. Remember that there's more than one car for sale, so if you're not happy about anything, go find another.

Chapter Eight

Owning and running

Without trying to put too fine a point on it, Evo ownership is definitely not a cheap business. Although it's a brilliantly-engineered, well-made Japanese car, with all of the benefits that come with those credentials, it isn't the most economical thing ever to hit the road. You have to look at the Evo in a slightly different light to almost any other saloon car. It might have four doors, five seats, and a decent size of boot, but you should be comparing running costs to something more like a big exotic sports car. Just remember the colossal levels of performance we're talking about.

Actually buying the vehicle in the first place shouldn't be too bad, depending on which model you go for. I'm not going to go through prices in this book because it'll be around for too long to have any relevance to something that will alter on a monthly basis. But the Evo does offer good value for money, particularly when you consider just how useful it is.

Unfortunately, actually buying the thing isn't the end of the expense, it's just the beginning. And the first thing that's going to start draining your wallet is insurance. This is going to be pretty hefty, and at the time of writing it was classified as Group 19 or 20, which is about as high as it gets. Also, just about all insurance companies will want some form of correctly fitted Thatcham-approved security device, so you could have to pay out a few more spons in order to get the theft cover you need. At least a decent alarm and tracking system should mean you keep hold of your new motor and stop it going walkabout.

Bearing in mind that the majority of the cars on the road are grey imports, you'll find that a lot of insurance companies won't even quote. For some reason – probably a lot to do with various TV-related witch-hunts on the deadly peril of buying a grey import – these companies don't want what they see as the hassle of insuring a car that doesn't have a full dealer/importer back-up. This is a bit ludicrous when you consider that Mitsubishi are providing decent spares availability, but since when did common sense play any part in vehicle insurance?

When you do find a quote, you must be prepared to tell the company about every mod you've done or has been done to your Evo, and it wouldn't hurt to tell them what plans you've got in store for it either. If you've used one of the specialists brokers recommended by other owners or the Mitsubishi Lancer Register scheme, you should have no problem talking to someone who knows what you mean when you start reeling off the list of tweaks, so you should end up with a sensible quote that takes everything in to consideration. Just remember to shop around and make sure you are comparing like for like when you get the figures. And whatever you do, don't tell any fibs about your previous history. All the companies are linked and if you don't mention previous accidents, losses, or convictions, they'll find out later and then you're in trouble.

So, with the car on the road and insured to the hilt, what's next? Well, the main thing you're going to feel is the fuel economy, or lack of it. You have to keep telling yourself that the engine under your bonnet can produce the thick end of 300bhp in standard form and that amount of power requires a certain amount of fuel, regardless of what size of motor is making it.

The problem – if that's the right word – seems to be that the power of an Evo is so accessible, and so very usable so much of the time, that you never just sit back and cruise. Every twist and turn in the road becomes something to be attacked, and every gap in the traffic becomes an opportunity to feel that rush of acceleration as you safely nip into a space other drivers could only dream about going for. Basically it's too much fun to not give it a bootful on a regular basis, so plan on getting a super unleaded account at your local filling station.

If you do cruise around in your Evo, watching the admiring glances that will undoubtedly come your way, the fuel economy still won't be great. Mid 20s are about as good as it gets, and when you start applying the accelerator with a bit of gusto you can easily hit the low teens – and worse. Add the small fuel tank into the equation and you can see why that petrol account might be a good idea.

OK, having thoroughly depressed anyone thinking about taking the plunge, let's move on to the servicing and ongoing maintenance tasks that an Evo owner should be looking at. This section isn't going to be a full-on 'How To' session on what to do during a full service on the various Evos that are available, because that would take up too much room. The idea of this bit is just to tell you what needs regular attention so that

Once you've got your Evo, get along to some shows and start talking to other owners. You'll find a wealth of knowledge out there to help you get the best from your car, and to find out about the best tuners, products, and suchlike.

you aren't let down by a failure, don't do any damage to something, and don't let a small problem become a major one. It's amazing how often a little item can be overlooked for a while, only for it to become a bigger – and more expensive – fault to rectify.

Now the first thing we're going to mention is keeping your Evo clean. Yes, we know it's a lot more fun to be out there driving it rather than running a soapy sponge over the bodywork, but it's really worthwhile doing. Not only will you keep your motor mint, but if you give your car a regular once-over you can spot small defects before they become major. Plus you'll get more admiring glances if you're driving something that's pristine rather than so filthy you can't see out of the windows, even if it does have a rally car pedigree.

Most of the things which need checking out are easy enough to do. Most important is engine oil level, which might sound a bit odd these days when we all expect engines not to leak oil and not to burn it either. Without wishing to state the obvious, make sure that you check the oil level when the car is on flat ground and wait at least five minutes after the engine has been turned off. So much oil remains in the top of the motor that if you don't wait for it to run back into the sump you'll get an incorrect reading on the dipstick. Don't forget, too much oil can damage an engine, so let the level settle before you check it. And remember to check it regularly, too.

Regardless of whether you stick to the Mitsubishi interval or change the oil every 3,000 miles (4,800km), make sure you give your motor a few litres of the really good stuff. A fully synthetic oil is an absolute necessity to keep the engine in top condition, so make sure you find a good one. Your tuning specialist should be able to recommend a decent brand, so once you've started using that one, stick to it.

It's a good idea to use genuine Mitsubishi oil filters, too. Most Evo specialists swear by them and, again, they won't break the bank. In fact, when you compare the price of a five-litre can of pukka synthetic oil and a good filter to the price of an engine rebuild, you'll see it's much cheaper to put top quality lubricant in there and keep things healthy.

Another thing to have a look at while you're under the bonnet is the engine coolant level. This is checked at the coolant expansion tank, which is marked with a high and low water line. The level should be checked with a cold engine and should, obviously, be above the low mark. Whatever you do, wait until the motor

has cooled down before you try and top up the bottle. If you need to do this you should use a water and antifreeze mix, or neat antifreeze, rather than plain water. Just adding water will eventually weaken the antifreeze strength until it becomes ineffective. Actually, calling the additional cooling fluid 'antifreeze' is a bit misleading. It not only prevents the fluid in the engine from freezing but also aids the cooling performance during the summer, and has additives that prevent corrosion forming in the system too.

The expansion tank is also a good place to check on the condition of your engine. Clean fluid tinged with the colour of the antifreeze additive generally means that all is well. If you are regularly topping up the fluid you must find out what is happening to the coolant, and rectify the fault before it becomes more serious. If the liquid appears to be getting murky and creamy, this is a sign that engine oil is getting into the coolant system somewhere, and this needs attention very quickly. Possible causes include head gasket failure, engine block or head problems, or water pump woes. All of these need proper diagnosis to find out what the root cause is, which should be dealt with as soon as is practicable.

While we're still looking around the engine bay, check your brake fluid reservoir. On Evos this is a bit of a swine to get to, so it can often be overlooked. By watching the level of the fluid and how much it needs topping up, you can see how your brakes are wearing. If you've put plenty of fluid in since your brakes were last looked at, they probably need a bit of attention. Otherwise you'll gouge some nice grooves into your discs and end up with brakes that won't do their job when you really need them to.

If you do any track-day sessions, make sure you check your pads before you go to the circuit, and if you are, shall we say, 'enthusiastic' in the way you attack the corners, check them through the day. I've seen people turn up at a circuit, put race-spec pads in, and then change them when they've worn them out during the day. They finish off by replacing the road-spec pads before they drive home.

Another thing that you should consider if you do a lot of track work is the possibility of warping your front discs through overheating them. The problem seems to be that after a few fast laps, the brakes have got very hot. Then the car comes into the pits, is parked up, and the discs begin to cool down at different rates. The exposed disc sheds heat quite quickly, but the bit

sandwiched between the pads remains scalding hot for longer, which can lead to the discs warping. If you get the chance, really use the 'cooling down' lap to do just that, and your brakes should have a better chance of survival.

Also, using track-only pads can mean that your discs become a service item, because race friction material is generally a lot more aggressive towards the disc. On the other hand, you'll be having so much fun, who cares if you're replacing discs on a regular basis? If you do stick to original-spec pads for most driving, it's worth noting that Evo I front pads are the same as Evo III and IV, but almost three times the cost. Buy the Evo III ones and save some dosh. Similarly, the Brembo pads fitted to Evo Vs and up are much more expensive when they come in a Mitsubishi box, so get them in a Brembo box and save a fortune.

When you're doing your weekly maintenance, don't forget hidden reservoirs like these tucked away in the boot.

Also, as a bit of a precaution, give the top of the reservoir a good wipe if you need to top it up. It saves any muck getting into the fluid which then goes on to damage the rest of the components. Something to remember about the braking system is that the fluid should be totally changed at least every two years. Brake fluid is hygroscopic, meaning it attracts moisture, and as the water content of the fluid builds up, the efficiency of the system goes down. Sticking to this two-year limit, or changing the fluid more often if you do lots of heavy motoring, is a very good idea.

On older Evos you will probably have a battery that requires attention, so give that a once-over whenever you check the oil and coolant. The Japanese-spec batteries are tiny, so they need to be in good nick to save any aggravation. Each cell will have a required fluid level mark on it and, if the level is low, it should be topped up with de-ionised water. This is available from motorists' stores and isn't expensive, so get the right stuff. If you use tap water you will end up contaminating the electrolyte and shortening the battery's useful life.

Again, the battery condition can be used as an indicator to show you how good or bad the charging system is. If the electrolyte level keeps dropping, but there isn't an actual leak from the battery casing, it probably means the charge rate is too high, and that the fluid is being boiled off. Accompanying symptoms can be furry battery terminals and even bleached paint around the battery area. Either check the charge rate yourself with a multi-meter, or go along to a decent auto-electrician and get him to look at it.

On later cars the battery is more likely to be a 'sealed for life' item, which is a bit of a misleading title. Every lead-acid battery going has some form of ventilation hole in case it needs to vent off hydrogen gas. The 'sealed' bit refers to the fact that you can't take the top off and add a drop of electrolyte if it's got a little low. They still suffer from being overcharged, in which case they, too, will fur their terminals and bleach your paintwork. If you have a battery with a vent-pipe nozzle, make sure there is a pipe fitted to it to direct the gases away under the car.

Whichever battery type you have on your Evo, remember that a lead-acid battery's performance degrades severely once it has been completely flattened. How you managed to flatten the battery is totally unimportant, but once it's been dragged down to the point where it won't even click your solenoid, it's effectively shot. If you do flatten the battery, find out why it happened, fix the fault if necessary, and get a new battery to make sure you aren't left stranded.

While you're looking at the charging system it's worth checking the alternator drivebelt. It's simple to test for adequate tightness and condition, and easy

DID YOU KNOW?

OK, we keep banging on about how thirsty Evos are, but let's consider how efficient they are instead. Almost 300bhp effectively costs 20mpg on average, but can you think of any 100bhp cars that do 60mpg? That makes Evos very efficient!

When it comes to servicing, make sure the work is done by an Evo specialist. There are plenty of them about, so ask around to get a few personal recommendations. Unless you're very handy with the spanners, it isn't really a DIY kind of car.

enough to adjust or replace. When checking the belt, look closely for any nicks or cuts in the rubber. These stress points are where belts fail, so if you find any frayed areas, change the belt.

Another area so often neglected these days is the condition and pressure of the tyres. According to various motoring organisations, one of the main reasons for accidents on the motorway is tyre failure, and when you watch how some people abuse their tyres, you can see why. When you remember how much stress the car can inflict on the rubber at each corner, it makes sense to ensure it's always in first-rate order.

As well as keeping the tyres up to the right pressure, check the condition of them regularly. The main problem to look for is uneven wear at the edges of the tyre tread. If the outside or inside edge appears to be wearing a lot more rapidly than the rest, the most likely answer is that there's a problem in the wheel alignment. This could be because things haven't been correctly realigned after brake or suspension work, or it might simply be that a wheel has been heavily kerbed and it's knocked the tracking out.

If you become a regular track-day hero, consider having another set of wheels and tyres purely for the circuit. It might seem like a hefty expense, but being able to turn up on good road rubber, then fit the other stuff for the sessions, makes a lot of sense. It also means you shouldn't get into the situation where you rip your tyres to shreds on the circuit and then have to run the gauntlet of the local plod on the way home before you can get the knackered rubber swapped.

Whatever the reason for uneven tyre wear, it needs sorting out as soon as possible. You aren't buying poxy remoulds from a cheap-and-cheerful joint, so make sure you get the best from them. As for finding the time to check your rubber, why not do it while you're cleaning your alloy wheels?

Finally, be aware of how your car feels when you drive it. Get used to the way it sounds, the way it responds to your steering and braking inputs, and how it performs. If you drive a car regularly you might not pick up on areas that deteriorate gradually as the miles clock up. Regular maintenance, and being tuned in to how your Evo feels, will help you to keep it in the best of health.

All things considered, an Evo in any form is going to be a bit of an expensive way to travel. While it can be practical and carry passengers and luggage, it'll be stiffly suspended, demanding to drive, and will need proper care and attention. So the question has to be, 'Is it worth all the hassle and expense?' Well, *duh!* Of course it is! If you haven't already done it, get out there and get one bought.

Oh, you'll have to get used to doing this a fair bit, but the fun of driving a car as wild as an Evo makes it worth it.

Chapter **Nine**

All it needs is more power!

The market for tuning and modifying cars is bigger today than it's ever been, and you only have to look at the motoring section of a newsagent's shelves to see that there are plenty of magazines devoted to all manner of mobile tweakery. And the overall impression given by a lot of these comics is that most people buy a popular car and then cover it in glass-fibre additions to try and make it look either totally different to the car they bought, or very much like something else. The thing is that for a lot of these mod monkeys, cosmetic considerations totally outweigh the practical and performance aspects of their cars.

When it comes to Mitsubishi Evolutions, though, things aren't often like that – thank goodness! Apart from a few cosmetic enhancements, most of the modification work is carried out under the skin, and it's generally done with one aim in mind: to make the car even more potent than it was when it left the factory.

To some tuners and owners this will mean a couple of bolt-on goodies that put a bit more spring in the Evo's step, but to others it will be a relentless pursuit of horsepower that can see the factory output doubled – and then some. To go with this, areas of the transmission are beefed up, the suspension is overhauled, and the braking system is brought into line with the new heights of performance.

To find out what can be done at different levels, I spoke to a few tuners who've been working their magic on Evos for years, and got their ideas on what works and – just as importantly – what doesn't. I also thought it would be worthwhile going over just how these tweaks actually work. For every enthusiast who knows engine and chassis tuning inside out, there are plenty of people who aren't really sure, and who don't really want to be the ones to raise their hands in class and ask

the questions. Hopefully, by reading this they won't have to.

Simple stuff

Of all the engine mods you can do, upgrading the air filter and exhaust system have to be two of the easiest tweaks. Swapping a panel filter is simplicity itself, and a full induction kit can be usually be fitted by the most ham-fisted individual in a matter of minutes. Even a new pipe is normally straightforward enough for anyone who can safely get under their car, and knows which end of the spanner to use.

So, if putting them on is dead easy, where's the catch? Are there any drawbacks to fitting these bits and, once you've done it, will your Evo perform any better? Let's look at air filters first and see what we can make out.

Air filters

Performance air filters can be broken down into three distinct types. Replacement panels are the first to consider, being a higher-flow version of the original item. The main advantages of replacement panels are that they are nice and quiet and they use the factory cool air ducting. Some versions can even be washed clean and reused.

The panels, just like the cone filters we'll come to in a minute, are generally made from either foam or oiled cotton gauze. You should be careful when choosing between the different material types because Evos aren't too keen on ingesting small particles of muck and grit through their turbos. Although the Evo airflow meter (AFM) doesn't get affected by any filter oil passing through it, any oil build-up in the trunking feeding the turbo can spell disaster. Minute particles of dirt can congregate together, using the oil as a binding agent.

Fitting a performance air filter like this **Blitz SUS** unit is pretty easy, but going to the trouble of swapping round the battery and filter on an Evo V or VI is worth the extra time and expense. It's much better to get plenty of cool air into the motor than leave it breathing hot stuff.

This Evo has been treated to an **HKS** Super Power Flow air filter and a full hard-pipe kit so that all the pressure created by the turbo gets into the engine. The new **HKS** dump valve is fitted just behind the filter on the boost pipe that goes to the inlet plenum.

Once the lump becomes big enough to break free from the trunking wall, it smashes into the compressor wheel, and bang goes the turbo. Even minute particles can wreak havoc on the turbine blades when they are spinning at colossal revs. Check just how good the filter is before you pay your dosh. This also holds true for cones and enclosed systems, so make sure whoever's selling you the bits can assure you your turbo won't hate you for what you're about to do.

Moving up from a new element you come to the all-new high-flow filter. Evos are afflicted with restrictive air boxes that are far better junked in favour of a decent free-flow filter. These cones will usually be part of kit which contains the correct brackets to make one a nice fit on the car, but some filters are a one-size-fits-all universal jobbie that will need some work to fit neatly.

These filters are available as the ubiquitous cone shape, or are more mushroom-shaped, depending on how the designers have decided to improve the airflow through the filter. Most designs have some sort of flow improvement ideas, either in the shape of the cone itself, or the neck that leads into the airflow meter, or both. The trick is to increase the airspeed and guide the fast-moving charge smoothly into the inlet tract.

Apart from their ability to flow a lot more air than the original 'box arrangement, these filters are much noisier than the standard items. To some people, this increase in volume is worth the price on its own, but if you enjoy driving with a bit more refinement you could find the constant sucking sounds from under the bonnet a bit wearing. Noises also differ between the filter elements, with a stainless steel mesh making a whistling noise totally unlike the throaty growl you'd get from a cotton element.

Adjustable cam pulleys can be very useful for dialling in the exact cam timing for the most power. You need someone who can check the results accurately to get the best from them, but if you're going for lots of motor upgrades they should be somewhere on the shopping list.

A more important issue with a new cone-type filter will be the possible lack of cool-air feed. If you buy a kit that includes ducting and panelling to keep warmed-up air away from the filter you should be fine, but just swapping to a cone that ends up breathing hot air could even end up costing you power rather than giving you more. Not really what you're after.

To get around this minor hiccup there are a couple of things you can do. Obviously you can cobble together some ducting to force cool air into the general area of the filter, and then rig up some heat shielding to keep the hot stuff out of the vicinity – you *can*, but unless you're a bit handy with the tools, it could easily look like a dog's dinner. On later cars a better idea would be to get a relocation kit that would swap the battery and filter around in the engine bay. This leaves the filter nearer the front of the car in a much cooler place. You can even get custom-made boxes that envelop the new filter in a sea of cold air, helping the engine's efficiency no end.

The last piece in the air filter jigsaw is the enclosed filter, which is an amalgam of cone filter and cold-air box. The idea is simple enough. A custom-made enclosure holds the filter, which is mounted on a suitable plate that bolts to the AFM. From the other end of the box comes a pipe that can be routed to the grille area or under the wheel arch. They aren't the cheapest alternative, and the kits are more universal, but they can do a good job of keeping the incoming charge cool.

One thing to keep an eye on if you do go for a new induction kit is how it affects your fuelling. In particular, part throttle settings can lean off, leading to a slight hesitancy through the mid-range before the power comes romping in at the top end. Before you decide which filter to go for, have a word with your friendly local tuning shop and get their advice on which is the best bet for your car.

Exhausting possibilities

On the other side of the four-stroke cycle, the exhaust manifold and system are equally important for top performance. And generally, a turbo'd engine just wants the least restriction possible after the turbine. One tuner I know even mentioned that no exhaust after the turbo would be the best idea, but I think that the noise, burnt paint in the engine bay, and constant tugs from PC Plod would get on your nerves in very short order.

Getting rid of any restrictions in the pipework after the turbo is obviously the best idea, and that means the original catalytic converter needs to find a new home. Most of the big Japanese tuning companies can provide performance cat-back systems that leave the cat in place, but other manufacturers make cat-bypass pipes

that give free flow all the way through. Bear in mind, however, that a car running without its cat may not pass MOT or roadside emissions tests.

Which pipe you go for obviously depends on the recommendations you get for what will work best on your car. After hearing a few horror stories about some stainless steel systems that rot out and fall apart in a matter of months, it's probably a good idea to check just how ironclad the 'lifetime warranty' really is. But if you go for a well-known and respected brand you shouldn't have any problems.

All you need to worry about is how loud the exhaust noise will be, and if you can live with it. The extra performance should be there regardless. It's worth noting that some pipes made from mild steel are actually a bit quieter in use than those made from stainless, and they don't drone as badly during steady speed work either.

Electronics

A few years ago, the accepted ideas of engine tuning generally boiled down to bigger carbs, lumpier cams, cutting as much port away out of the cylinder head as was practical, and then sticking an extractor exhaust manifold on that would use the exhaust pulses to draw more gases after them. In the world of tuning modern Japanese performance engines, the same results are achieved in a more scientific and electronically-enhanced way.

This ARC manifold cover looks much nicer than the stock item, but just what does that slogan mean? Answers on a postcard, please...

Before we go on to the modifications let's talk a little about what engine management units – also known as Electronic Control Units or ECUs – do. Basically, these units monitor what is happening in the engine by the use of various sensors. Then they make sure the correct amount of fuel arrives at the right time, and that it is ignited with a spark when it is safe to do so, based on the information they receive from the sensors.

The more complicated the management system, the more sensors it monitors, and the more information is taken into account before the fuel and spark are delivered. On a turbocharged engine like the 4G63 the ECU will also look after the boost pressure, and amend that in conjunction with everything else it's controlling, to give the best combination of power output, fuel economy, and engine longevity. How clever is that?

This information received from the sensors is referenced against the map that is contained in the ECU. This map will have been developed to give what the manufacturer considers to be the best compromise between the requirements just mentioned, at any given rev point, under any given situation. If you want more power, but don't mind sacrificing a few mpg or ultimately knowing that your engine might not last as long as standard, this map can be amended to suit.

Inputs come from sensors that read how far the throttle is open, how much airflow is going into the motor, air and engine temperature, engine speed, crank position, and fuel mixture, giving the ECU a complete picture of what the engine is doing and what is being expected of it. On later OBDII-equipped cars there's another lambda sensor and a Manifold Absolute Pressure (MAP) sensor that detects manifold vacuum, but these are both used for emissions control.

Getting around the standard map's parameters can be done in a couple of ways, by either adding one or more dedicated adjustable electronic boxes, or by completely removing the standard ECU and fitting one that's programmable to suit your engine's needs. What you go for depends on how much more you want from your Evo, and the level of tune of the rest of the engine.

Until recently, the Japanese way of tweaking their motors was to add piggyback modules into the wiring loom between sensors and ECU. These boxes would intercept the sensor outputs, and then modify or delete the signal that was sent on to the original ECU and get it to behave in a non-standard way. On a turbocharged engine, that meant a standard ECU could be fooled into allowing more ignition advance, longer injector duty cycles, and more boost, because the signals the ECU received were telling it something slightly different to what was actually going on.

Some modules, like boost controllers, come with ancillary mechanical components that replace standard parts in the engine bay. These work in conjunction with the new brain to give power outputs beyond the capability of the original items but, by careful setting-up, they can increase the performance without significantly reducing motor life.

These add-ons are a sure way to get more power from a motor but, unless they are set up correctly, they can also turn it into a short-fused bomb. Their ease of adjustability means that some people just can't resist playing with them, and when something is taken outside safe limits – say fuelling leaned off too much or boost run too high – the motor can melt down.

There are modules on the market that let you tweak any aspect of your engine's performance, and several can handle more than one function, so you might only need one box of tricks to do what you need. Boost controllers are available that allow you to toggle between two or more boost settings to suit driving conditions, and most have a short-duration setting which allows maximum power for quick blasts before it

Getting the fuel mixture right is absolutely critical to performance and engine safety. Here a lambda probe has been attached to the exhaust to give an accurate reading of what's coming out of the motor.

drops back to the pre-set boost point. The standard boost solenoid is replaced with an uprated one that alters the boost signal going from the boost source on the turbo compressor to the wastegate, based on what the controller tells the solenoid to do.

Fuel computers can be added to increase fuelling all through the rev range, or at specific areas where the standard set-up runs out of steam, so to speak, and ignition computers allow a tweak of the ignition curve to match the motor's new requirements. The only problem with these add-on modules is that they are generally more coarse in their operation and set-up, and they've always got the 'itchy finger' problem we've already mentioned.

Don't forget that you can overdo things. This motor went pop because too much boost got through when the wastegate stuck shut. The hole was made by a scared con rod that didn't like being in the dark any more.

At a similar level – but one that doesn't have all the associated problems of untutored fingers playing with dangerous buttons – are new vehicle-specific ECUs that can be pre-programmed to work with the engine's modifications, and then hidden away out of sight. While something like this isn't as flash as having complex-looking boxes on the dashboard, such ECUs are often a safer bet for someone who can't resist having a quick fiddle to see what happens. Several engine tuners I've spoken to like these units because they are fit-and-forget, and can't be abused.

Recently, though, a more specialised product in the form of the race-bred ECU has become available, and

with the right software almost any engine set-up can be configured. Rather than relying on a tuner adjusting a few settings on a curve, and then using the unit to interpolate the positions between the chosen points, these new units can be fully mapped to give exactly the right amounts of fuel, ignition, boost and so on at any point on the rev band, just like the factory ECU. Obviously, these units were really designed for race use, but as tuners develop higher levels of road engine tweakery the sophistication needed from the engine management increases so that it can keep everything running at peak performance without problems. That's why well-tweaked road cars are ending up running fully-mappable ECUs.

A good tuner can programme a three-dimensional map that looks after fuelling, and another map for ignition to make sure that any combination of speed, gear, temperature, and boost is precisely catered for.

There are several systems out there that offer this multi-layered option in fine engine system control, so you have plenty of choice as to what level you go to, and which equipment you opt for. Which one is right for you is the $64,000 question. It's one best answered by the tuner who can quantify your needs, and then sell you the right product to go with them. All you have to do is find the right tuner.

Fuelling

No matter what Evo model you're driving, there's something that you'll use that's just the same as everyone else – regardless of engine tuning or how you use the car, you'll have to stick some fuel in there every now and again to make it go. Well, probably more often than that, but you get my meaning.

Although UK-spec Evos can get away with guzzling the cheapest unleaded juice, and do so without damaging their motors, not all the Japanese imports are happy doing that. In fact, if you drive a newly-imported car on the lowest octane-rated fuel you stand a risk of doing your engine a serious mischief before you realise.

Back home in Japan, 100 octane fuel is the norm, whereas over here premium unleaded is 95, and super is between 97 and 98 octane. If you don't have the mods done to allow the use of the lower-rated stuff, you can burn valves and melt pistons in very short order. Of course, you can raise the octane rating of the fuel you put in by using an octane booster, but this is more usually reserved for playtime on track days, when the motor will be working very hard for comparatively long periods of time.

One interesting point worth mentioning is that an octane booster – or a higher octane fuel – doesn't give you an appreciable difference in power output. Instead, a higher octane rating will give more protection against detonation, and therefore engine damage, but it isn't the power booster that most people seem to think it is. Running a higher-octane fuel like Shell Optimax simply helps your engine to avoid detonation, and that will stop the engine management from retarding the ignition timing and robbing you of a few bhp. The protection given by the better fuel just lets you access the full power the engine is designed to produce for more of the time – it doesn't give you any extra power at all.

If you actually want to get more horsepower from your engine by feeding it different fuel, you can use a specialist race mix that is designed to run with the type of motor you're using, but there are a few drawbacks. Not only is it much more expensive than road fuel – anything up to five or six times the cost at the time of writing – but once you've had your engine management reprogrammed to suit, you can't go back to standard pump gas.

Once you've got your Evo running on the correct grade of fuel for best performance and longevity, you're probably going to start thinking about getting a bit more power from the motor. When you do that you're going to have to increase the amount of fuel available to the engine so that it can efficiently burn more and so give the required boost in performance. For mild increases you'll probably find that the original equipment fuelling gear will be able to supply enough extra juice to do the job, but you don't have to go too far before the cracks start showing – literally!

One of the first things to consider upgrading is the fuel pump and its power feed. On Evos you can increase the amount of fuel simply by getting a better voltage feed through to the original pump. You run heavy-duty cable direct from the battery to the pump, via a relay controlled by the existing fuel pump wiring. You could change the fuel pump instead, but the wiring is a more simple job that doesn't involve getting up to your elbows in 97RON.

The next step is to fit a fuel pressure regulator that can be tweaked to make sure there's just the right amount of juice available for the injection system. That little tweak should be enough to keep up with the fuel demands up to 400bhp on later cars (from the Evo V on) that run larger injectors. If you go much further than that with the mods, then you can count on fitting an

An uprated fuel pressure regulator should be part of a tuned Evo's spec, allowing more flow at a higher pressure to meet increased demands.

uprated pump that can supply much more Super than the stocker, even working flat out.

Like fuel pumps, the fuel rail and the injectors can also need increasing in size. Just how far you uprate these bits depends on the state of tune you want to move up to, but if you're asking for big power, you'd better be ready to squirt lots of fuel into the cylinders. Your friendly tuning specialist will be able to advise exactly what is needed on your motor for the planned mods.

Although they look pretty similar, the high-flow fuel pump on the left can push a lot more fuel into the Evo's system than the original jobbie on the right.

The general rule is to go bigger than you need and then turn down the injectors' duty cycle so that they release the right amount of fuel for the engine tune. This means they've got the additional capacity to keep up with a thirstier motor at a later date. A small injector running 97 per cent duty cycle has no additional capacity for tuning, but a bigger injector running 65 per cent has plenty to go at when you're ready for the next step. Generally, injector prices are very similar, so why not buy the bigger ones and then turn them down a bit?

So, what do you need to look after these bigger injectors? All this extra flow capacity is nothing without some form of control to make sure the right amount of juice is getting into the combustion chamber at the right time. The vehicle's engine management computer tells the injectors when to open, and how long to remain open for – ie, the duty cycle; all you have to do is get the computer to hold the injectors open for the right amount of time for any given fuel demand.

The usual Japanese way of altering the fuel control is to piggyback an extra module onto the original ECU so that the signals coming from the engine are intercepted and then amended. This way the ECU delivers the required duty cycle signal without thinking that the engine is running outside regular parameters. This is fine up until you hit a point where the signal needed isn't available in the ECU's standard map. Then you have to move on to something more sophisticated.

This means moving up to a totally new, programmable ECU that you can have mapped to give exactly the right duty cycle under any combination of engine conditions. Both the piggyback fuel computer and the replacement ECU will need specialist programming, but they are the only way to get your fuelling matched correctly to your engine's state of tune. And if the programmer is switched on, you could even see slightly better fuel economy. Then get ready for some serious fun, and yet more visits to the filling station.

Turbos

Turbochargers are a device that every pub expert knows everything about, but when you start quizzing them in depth the answers get a bit shaky. Well, hopefully, once you've read this you should be able to make Billy No Mates down the boozer shut up once and for all. And you should be able to make a more informed choice if you come to upgrade your turbo, and be able to keep the one you have on top form too.

First of all we should probably look at what a turbocharger actually is and the basic theory of how it does what it does. To explain it in its most elemental form, a turbo is made up of a pair of finned wheels attached to opposite ends of a shaft, and these wheels run inside snail-like housings. One of these housings is connected to the exhaust manifold, so the gases that exit the engine pass over the fins of the first wheel, spinning it up to a speed that depends on the amount and velocity of the gas flowing over it.

The compressor wheel that's bolted to the opposite end of the shaft spins equally fast in the intake air stream. This pulls air into the system and pressurises it as it heads for the engine, force-feeding the cylinders with more charge than would be possible under atmospheric pressure. Simple. And the pressurisation is done using the energy that was being thrown away down the exhaust, so it really is something for nothing. Well, almost.

Unfortunately nothing really is that simple, and there are lots of variables that affect how the turbo works and how it integrates with the rest of the engine tuning package. There are also a couple of different ways of actually putting the thing together and, not surprisingly, each method has its advocates. Let's start getting a bit more serious.

Mix and match

To make the 'charger work efficiently over the range that the motor has been designed for, a turbo designer has to consider a lot of different factors. If the installation is going onto a road engine that's designed for a good spread of everyday power, the turbo will have to give strong mid-range and top end power without being too 'laggy', making the engine asthmatic in the lower rev range.

On the other hand, if the engine is going into a top-end track weapon, then power in the upper rev range is all that counts, and the driver will just have to get used to frantically working the gearbox to keep the engine spinning fast enough. The lag that would be unsuitable for a road car isn't really a consideration.

Getting the right response from the turbocharger depends on matching the sizes of the turbine and compressor wheels, and the housings they work in. On a road engine – which is probably what we should concern ourselves with for now – and in an ideal world, a turbo will show no lag, usefully aid an engine in the lower mid-range, and get progressively stronger as the revs rise. By the time the engine has reached its redline, the turbo will be getting close to its maximum

Above: This is what you get when you buy a GReddy T25 turbo kit, complete with external wastegate, pipework and new tubular manifold. The straight black pipe is the wastegate outlet, which dumps exhaust gas from the system when full boost is reached. No silencer means that this conversion can be very loud on full throttle, but it sounds fantastic!

Below: Here's the assembled kit, showing the exhaust gas path into and out of the turbo, and how the wastegate hooks up to the manifold.

And here's one in place, with a new air filter and a race recirculating dump valve that feeds excess pressurised air back into the air intake.

flow rate, but not actually holding the engine back.

If the turbo isn't sized correctly, various problems can appear. If it's simply too big for the engine it might only just be getting into its stride by the time the engine is at its peak revs, making the car a gutless performer. But if the turbo is too small, it will run out of boost before the engine is maxed out and will be actually holding the revs back. Getting the application bang-on is a difficult balancing act, but drive a standard Evo – particularly a late model – and you'll see that it can be done really well.

'Gates and valves

While you're taking all this in, there are another couple of components to consider. The first is the wastegate, and the second is the blow-off or dump valve. These two items combine to control the boost pressure operating on the engine. Boost control is needed for three reasons. The first is to limit the turbo's pressure output and prevent damage to the motor. Secondly, the turbo needs reining in to stop it running too fast and damaging itself. And finally, the boost characteristics of the turbo system need matching to the needs of the engine.

The wastegate works in conjunction with its actuator to govern the maximum amount of boost that can be provided by the turbo. The actuator is linked pneumatically to the pressure being created in the inlet manifold, so once boost pressure gets to a pre-set level, the actuator begins to open the wastegate. This allows some of the exhaust gas to bypass the turbo and prevent it producing any more boost. The clever trick is to make the actuator do this while allowing the turbo to continue producing the maximum level of boost without any unwanted drop-off, boost surge, or spikes.

The dump valve works on the intake side of the engine and vents the pressurised air in the boost piping when the throttle is shut and the air has nowhere else to go. If this pressure isn't released it can stall the turbo, because the compressed air has to go somewhere, and if it can't go through the throttle it'll head back through the compressor housing. This can cause lots of damaging stress to the turbine wheel. By venting this air outside the pressurised system, the turbo can keep spinning, and, when the throttle is reopened, the pressure quickly rises up and off you go again.

This is one of the pair of intercooler water jets fitted as standard to spray cooling water onto the intercooler core and lower the intake air temperature. The centre jet is part of a computer-controlled system that fires the water automatically to augment the standard system.

On the Evolution the dump valve is a recirculating type, meaning it sends the vented air back into the inlet tract, upwind of the turbocharger. This helps to minimise the lag once the throttle is reopened and it also stops the stalling problems associated with some atmospheric dump valves. These are the ones that make that mad whooshing and hissing sound as they work, but, although they sound cool, can cause you problems.

Keeping your cool

One nasty by-product of the pressurisation of the incoming air charge is the way it's heated up. This would lower the efficiency of the motor if something wasn't done to cool down the air to as close to the ambient temperature of the air outside the engine bay as possible.

To do this, an air-to-air radiator – called an intercooler – is fitted into the intake system so that the compressed air is passed through the intercooler core and the temperature is lowered by the flow of air going across the core. It works in exactly the same way as the car's water radiator, and on the Evo the intercooler is fitted just inside the front bumper.

Thankfully, the intercooler is good enough on the Evos not to need replacement until the tuning level reaches the thick end of 400bhp. Unfortunately, the piping that leads to and from it is another matter. Once the power level gets much above the mid 300s the pipes need changing to bigger diameter ones for better flow. This is essential over 350bhp.

Variations on a theme

While a lot of turbocharger internals are made from steel or aluminium, you will often see the words 'ceramic' and 'titanium' bandied about. Ceramic doesn't crop up on Evos, although titanium turbos are fitted to Makinens and some RS models. But titanium turbos aren't completely titanium at all; only the exhaust turbine wheel is. The rest of the unit is made from conventional steel, aluminium, and cast iron.

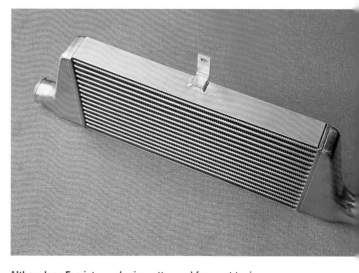

Although an Evo intercooler is pretty good for most tuning applications, once the power demands get towards 400bhp a new, larger intercooler is required.

With a lot more power to play with, the clutch can often need upgrading. This Exedy twin-plate system comes complete with a new flywheel and can hold onto 450bhp.

The benefit of using titanium for the turbine is that it's lighter and spins up faster, aiding turbo response. Quite whether you can tell the difference between titanium and standard on the road is another matter. The downside is that these turbines are more fragile than their steel counterparts and catastrophic failure isn't unknown at very high track-induced temperatures.

Another buzz phrase at the moment is 'roller bearing turbo'. Building a turbo with roller bearings on the central shaft instead of plain bearings can help the turbo to react faster to increased gasflow, but again it can be difficult to tell the difference during normal or even spirited driving. Track use might show up the slightly faster response better, but most drivers would struggle to notice it.

A tuned Evo should have a few more gauges to monitor the engine systems and alert the driver to any problems. Unfortunately, putting them down in the centre console means they could be overlooked during serious driving sessions.

The big problem with roller bearing turbos is that they're non-repairable, meaning that if you allow your oil to get a little old and dirty, you run the risk of wearing out the bearings very quickly, and then you're faced with a bill to replace the whole unit instead of just getting them remanufactured. You pays your money...

As you'll probably read in some magazine feature articles, many people change the turbo on their car as part of an overall tuning package, and because of this there are plenty of people who will supply a turbo that has been modified to take account of an engine's upgrades. These modded turbos are generally called hybrids, and the builders mix and match housings and wheels to get the correct characteristics to go with the new engine requirements.

As well as changing the flow capability and response of the turbo, other jobs are carried out to increase either the durability or performance of the hybrid. Larger, 360° bearings can be fitted to the compressor-end of the shaft to better support it as the pressure builds up. The usual bearing only supports the shaft at three points around 270°, so the extra point of location can be very important in a heavily-loaded turbo.

When you consider that a small automotive turbo can spin at speeds well over 200,000rpm, you can appreciate that a minute stress on a small component can quickly become violent enough to cause total failure. Considering what they have to put up with, turbos really are remarkably durable.

Make it last

To get the best performance and life from the Mitsi's turbocharged engine, there are a few rules that you should learn and then stick to. The most important ones concern the engine oil and proper warm-up and cool-down techniques.

Because the turbine bearings have so much to put up with, they must be fed a healthy supply of scrupulously clean oil. Any minor contaminant particles can rip through a bearing surface and begin the turbo's demise, so make sure you use a good quality oil and change it every 3,000 miles (4,800km), as well as after every track session if you want your turbo to last more than weeks.

And make sure you don't mix semi-synthetic and synthetic oils either. The additional detergent in fully synthetic oil can loosen the small killer particles and send them on their way to the bearings, ready to do their worst. If you've just got your Evo try and find out what oil has been used in the engine, and as long as it's good stuff, stick to it.

With regard to warming up and cooling down the turbo, just use a bit of common sense. Don't beat the motor's brains out before it's reached the proper working temperature, otherwise the turbo will struggle to get the right amount of oil protection at the higher revs. And if you've been out caning the car around your favourite bit of twisty country roads, drive a couple of miles at steady speed to let the turbo cool down to a more regular temperature. This way the bearings aren't so hot that they cook the oil that sits in the turbo core once the motor is turned off.

And if you haven't got a turbo timer fitted, for goodness sake don't do that annoying little blip of the throttle before flicking the ignition key off. This really is the way to kill a turbo in very short order as it accelerates to high speed on the blip, and then it spins down without any oil being pumped through its bearings because the engine has already stopped turning. Please don't blip – it's not big, it's not clever, and it will cost you a fortune in the end.

To really baby your turbo you might think about fitting a turbo timer or even a remote-start car alarm. The turbo timer will keep the motor running for a pre-set time after you have turned off the ignition, allowing the turbo to cool down with plenty of oil circulating its internals. The remote starter helps because while you're finishing that extra cup of coffee with your bowl of wheaties, the engine is warming up steadily before you hit the cut and thrust of the traffic. Look after your turbo and it should give miles of useful and enjoyable service. Abuse it and it will fall apart and tear a big hole through your wallet.

Different stages

So, having given you some background about what the options are, and what everything does, what can you do to an Evo to get more power out of it? Well, it's probably best if we break that down into Evo I–III and then The Rest. This is because the earlier cars are more scarce, and they are slightly different in their make-up, as well as not quite as robust in the engine department. Start to look for big horsepower from an early Evo and you're into much bigger bills, because you've got more work to do to get the motor ready to rumble. So, without further ado...

Evo I–III

You can break down the tweaking process into three simple stages for early Evos and, if it's done properly, you won't have to go over the same area more than once to get the right end result. Just bear in mind that you should

be realistic with your requirements. So, think just how far you want to go with tuning before you start.

If you think you might go the whole way and have large amounts of engine work done, don't scrimp at any of the early stages or you'll just have to spend more cash than you needed to. Also, at the time of writing there wasn't a mappable ECU available to fit the earlier cars, so you have to play with the additional fuel and boost computers to release the extra power. If you want to get really big power, maybe you should be looking at doing things to a newer car.

Stage one

The first job is to increase the airflow through the motor, so you should be looking at a decent induction kit and a less restrictive exhaust. The best gain comes

A popular gauge mounting position is on the A pillar. This puts the gauge almost in the driver's eye-line, but it isn't too distracting.

This is a catalytic converter bypass pipe, or de-cat pipe. If you fit one, keep hold of your cat for MOT time. And if you're buying a car that's already got one fitted, make sure you get the cat from the seller. If he hasn't got it, you're into big money to replace it.

from getting rid of the restrictive catalytic converter, so make sure you get a de-cat pipe when you do the system. Together, these mods should give around 15–20bhp on an early Evo, with a small rise in boost pressure resulting from less exhaust restriction. The factory ECU should cope without any problem.

Stage two

This time we need to up the fuel delivery, and raise the boost pressure to around 1.3bar as well. An additional fuel computer can handle the extra fuelling control, and an uprated pump or pump wiring mod can provide the additional flow rate. The rise in boost should either be achieved with an adjustable mechanical boost control – but not a bleed valve, please – or a dedicated electronic boost controller.

You'll also need to fit some better spark plugs that can handle the higher temperatures without melting, but get this done properly and you should see an additional 40–50bhp. That's a useful increase in something as nimble as an Evo I.

Stage three

This is as far as the experts I spoke to wanted to go without doing major work on the bottom end of the motor, which would be prohibitively expensive on most cars as it would cost more than they had. So, a sensible third stage would involve a swap of camshafts and a change to vernier cam pulleys, as well as fitting a thicker metal head gasket.

The new cam pulleys would allow the cams to be dialled in exactly for the best power output, and the head gasket would let boost be raised to around 1.5–1.6bar without causing any internal difficulties. The jobs done in stage one would really be paying dividends now, with the engine breathing harder through the intake and exhaust, but not suffering any strangulation. An increase of around 80bhp should be on the cards for a motor like this, and it shouldn't have any detrimental effect on engine life as long as it's serviced and looked after properly.

Evo IV–VIII

Moving on to the newer cars we can consider them together, as things are very similar throughout the motors. The only real area of difference is on the Evo IV, which would need a bit more engine work if you were contemplating going for a power figure over 400bhp. In all honesty, I'd recommend you find your own tuner who you're happy with before you decide to go this far, so get talking to other Evo owners to find out who they'd recommend, then go and quiz the tuners about your requirements.

Stage one

As far as the first step goes on the later cars, it's the same as the early ones. Get the breathing sorted out and, if you're planning on going much further, consider using a battery relocation kit to get the air filter down behind the headlight in the cooler airstream. A power output around 310bhp should be available with this level of tune, and that makes for some serious cross-country fun, I'll tell you.

Stage two

Now we get a bit more serious and consider the engine management system. Although you could stay with auxiliary computers and get some good results, it wouldn't be far different in cost to get a mappable ECU and have the whole package of engine control in one box. If you want a user-tweakable boost controller this would have to go on top of the ECU, but that way you'd have the choice of fast, very fast, and 'Oh Mother!' Whichever route you take, the boost figure can be raised to 1.4bar, and an uprated fuel pump can supply the extra juice. With better spark plugs and a good mapping session, the car should be kicking out around 350bhp.

Above: This pair of A'PEXi auxiliary computers look after the boost and fuelling on a tweaked Evo VI. Although they are very sophisticated piggyback units, they can't be as tuneable as a new programmable ECU.

Below: These auxiliary gauges fill out the centre console along with an A'PEXi ignition computer and a Blitz Power Meter.

Above: Here's RC Developments tweaking an A'PEXi Power FC replacement ECU with the Power FC Commander. A laptop can also be used to do this, but the Commander is easier to keep in the car should a tweak be needed.

Stage three

Now we're starting to get a bit more serious. The motor gets some attention in the form of cams and vernier pulleys, together with competition head studs and a thicker metal head gasket to contain the increased pressure. On an Evo IV–VI you'll at least have to swap the lower boost pipe, and a full set would definitely help.

This flattened pipe is one of the standard boost pipes on an Evo V. Once the boost is increased it needs changing for a better one to remove the restriction from the airflow.

With the boost raised again, this time to 1.6bar, another 30bhp should be on the cards, meaning the Evo is being dragged around by 380bhp. That's a tidy amount which should give plenty of fun with good engine longevity, and not too unpleasant fuel economy when you're cruising. That last one's relative, by the way.

Stage four

This is the point where the standard turbo bows out, and a new turbocharger and tubular manifold appears on the scene. Because of the way the Mitsubishi manifold and turbo are designed, there's no scope to just slap a bigger turbo onto the original manifold flange and enjoy higher boost. That's why you need the full kit that comes with a new manifold. You'll also need to move up to something like 800cc injectors to keep up with the motor's new thirst.

Get this package fitted and, once the ECU has been suitably tweaked to compensate, you should have around 440bhp to play with. Given the levels of grip and safety provided by the quality of the late-model Evo's running gear, this makes for a very quick motor, on the road or the track. And it still remains reasonably user-friendly, so you don't have to suffer for your fun.

If you're serious about going to much higher levels than this you need to talk to a respected tuner, face to face, and be prepared to sell some family silver to cover the cost. As a bit of a taster I've got a few details on

DID YOU KNOW?

Although you can get your Evo out on track, that won't tell you how much power it's producing. But the Evo Club often run rolling road sessions where you can strap your car to the rollers and find out an exact figure. It's not as much fun as a track day, but there's still plenty of good-natured rivalry going on.

what is – at the time of writing – the most powerful Evo in the country at over 700bhp, where about the only thing still recognisable in the engine bay is the cam cover. Built by Norris Designs with the specific task of beating all comers at the Elvington 'Ten Of The Best' event in summer 2003, it uses a 2.2-litre JUN engine, monster turbo, huge injectors and race ECU, and a host of other uprated and rebuilt bits to get the power without turning itself into an expensive external combustion engine.

At the time of writing this was the most powerful Evo in the UK. Built by Norris Designs, it was fitted with a 2.2-litre JUN engine, monster turbo, and huge fuel-delivery system, working together to produce over 700bhp. Gulp! (Peter Robain)

Chapter Ten

Getting a grip

All the extra power obtained by tuning the engine is useless if you can't actually get it onto the floor and use it to move the car. So you should consider uprating the clutch in line with the mods you have planned and the use you're going to give the car. Fast road driving, and even a bit of circuit work, can be coped with by a standard clutch if you haven't gone for big power upgrades and you don't do full-bore drag starts at traffic lights.

If you do want to compete in the odd drag race you'll need to swap the original clutch, as it doesn't like gripping at high revs on fast starts. And if you're going for monster power, you'll definitely need to fit something heavy-duty enough to take the punishment. These are your options.

For mild mods, and spirited driving, you could change to an uprated organic clutch which would give you a better friction plate and the ability to handle more power, as well as remaining very driveable. The next step would be a paddle clutch, complete with new cover and flywheel, which would be capable of holding on to much more power and abuse. The only downside of a paddle clutch is that a lot of them are designed for competition applications, which can make them a bit of a pig to use in a street car. However, there are paddle set-ups out there that are designed for road use and are much easier to live with, so if you want to go down that route make sure your tuner knows what you want and can get you the right bit.

If you're going much further with power output – say over 400bhp from a motor with a new turbo – you need to think about a twin-plate clutch. This is the same basic idea as a paddle clutch, but there's a second friction plate and a floating plate between the two friction plates. This gives more surface area for the power to be passed through, so the clutch can hold on to more welly without throwing its hand in. The triple-plate clutch – necessary if you've got much more than 500bhp to grapple with – is bigger and heavier-duty than the twin, and generally not that nice to drive on the street. Still, if you've got that much power to play with, how much street driving are you going to do?

Braking

Having made your Evo faster than standard, it might be a good idea to look at what you can do to make it stop a bit quicker too. Some would say you should really do this before increasing the speed potential of a car, so let's be all virtuous, responsible, and sensible and sort it now.

The great thing is that Evo brakes are pretty good as standard, and the ones on the Evo V and later are stonking Brembo items; but there's always room for improvement. The earlier cars need most work, but what you do depends on how much you've increased the car's performance, and what you do with it when you're behind the wheel. Regular road use, including a blatt down your favourite set of twisties, can be helped by a set of better pads and maybe a disc swap, although if you spend every weekend on the ragged edge at the track, your OE-spec brakes will need help. But you'll find that out as soon as your brakes warp and fade and you end up in the kitty litter.

For early cars the first step of changing to an upgraded fast road pad will probably give you a noticeable benefit, with better friction giving improved braking performance. The slight downsides are generally that the pads can be a bit noisier, and they probably won't last as long as the original equipment items. I have to say 'probably' because the wear really depends on the amount of use the brakes get, but given that they feel better and stop you quicker, you're

If the original brakes aren't good enough, you can go for bigger stoppers like these AP Racing six-pot calipers. Just make sure your wheels have enough clearance to fit over the bits and you'll have tremendous stopping power.

as long as the car. Brake fluid is also an area where you can get improvements, but mainly from changing it regularly so that the effects of heat and vapour locking don't reduce braking efficiency.

And for road use, stick to a good DOT 4 fluid rather than a silicone-based DOT 5. This can eat away at rubber seals and give you problems with fluid leaks over time. While the DOT 4 might not be quite as high-performance as DOT 5, you'll be changing it every year – or sooner if you're often found on the track – and you probably won't notice the difference.

The next step from a pad swap is to fit performance discs, which normally means they're going to be either drilled or grooved, or sometimes both. Changing to something like this isn't quite the straightforward job that you might think, and what you end up using is even more dependent on the vehicle's use than the pad swap.

After talking to a few brake gurus, the same sort of feeling came up when discussing the merits of grooving and drilling discs. In most cases, the best brake performance comes from the disc that has the largest surface area. That means a plain, vented disc. Machining lots of grooves onto the disc face, or drilling it full of holes, cuts down the surface area, meaning that there is less friction material pressing against the disc at any one time. When a rotor is full of holes and slots, the pads have to be pressed harder against the disc to achieve the same amount of stopping power as an unmachined one.

So why do the drilling and grooving thing at all? Well, the idea behind grooves in the disc face is that they constantly deglaze the pad material and disperse brake dust, meaning it always gives the best performance. Drilling a disc helps it to cool quicker under stress, but considering that you have to work a drilled disc harder to achieve the same braking effort as a plain or lightly grooved disc, you can probably understand that it's going to get hotter to start with. Drilled ones are often a lot more noisy too.

So what's the best idea for a road disc that's suitable for all conditions? The general consensus seems to point to a lightly grooved disc with something like four or six slots that keep the pad in top form but don't sacrifice surface area or stress the disc so that it begins cracking under heavy use. Yep, that's another slight problem that drilled discs can suffer from if the going becomes too heavy.

If you do decide to go the whole hog and fit some monster discs and new calipers, you still have a couple

probably going to lean on them a bit harder. If you do, they won't last as long.

The Japanese-manufactured pads and discs seem to work best on the early cars, but be warned – they are pretty expensive. They do perform a lot better, though, so the expense is justified.

While we're at the simple end of the scale, think seriously about swapping the standard rubber flexy hoses for braided stainless steel ones. The gain in pedal feel is often worth the money straight away, and the fact that they don't balloon or perish means they often last of things to be wary of before you part with your hard-earned wedge. The main one has to be the suitability of the caliper for year-round road use. This covers both the material and design of the caliper as well as the way it works. If there are no dirt seals, or the caliper's made to be stripped and cleaned after every race, it's not going to last long with road car servicing intervals or by being covered in road grime and salt.

You should also find out just how progressively the caliper reacts to pedal pressure. If it's a road design you should be able to press the brakes lightly and slow up gently, or stamp on the pedal and stop rapidly. Race calipers are often 'all or nothing' designs that almost turn the pedal into an on-off switch, which isn't suitable for regular motoring. If you do go for a full set-up, choose something that can take the different stresses of road use.

On an Evo IV you can swap to the front Brembo set-up from the later cars and enjoy the better braking that they have, but you can go even further if you still feel short of stopping power.

Bearing the previous comments in mind, a big brake combination using a six-pot caliper and something like a 330mm or 362mm disc will give you as much retardation as you should need. Just make sure, if you're planning on lots of road use, that the pad compound you choose is suitable for street driving and doesn't need to be heated up before it starts working. Oh, and check that they'll actually fit under your wheels – not from the diameter, but the width. It sounds daft, but there are plenty of fat calipers that might cause you problems if your wheel spokes run pretty close to the original caliper. You have been warned.

After thinking about all these options for the front brakes, you might be wondering what to do with your rear anchors. Basically, you shouldn't do that much, otherwise you'll upset the balance that the manufacturer carefully engineered into the car at the design stage. A new set of discs and pads should do the back end proud without the need to go to a twin-cylinder master cylinder that you can balance to compensate for the over-braked rear end. If you over-brake the rear end, you could be doing unexpected 360s just when you need to be totally in control.

Whichever upgrades you decide to go for, make sure they are carried out by someone who knows what they're doing. Out of all the things you can do to a car, playing with the brakes gives you the least margin for error, so an incorrectly tightened bolt or missed

retaining clip can have disastrous effects. Get them sorted correctly and you'll be both quicker *and* safer, which is what it's all about.

Suspension

Of all the mechanical upgrades you can do to a car, uprating the suspension seems to be one of the blackest of the black arts. Everyone can appreciate big turbos, fancy engine electronics, or big brake systems, but those funny tube things covered with a spring and stuck behind each wheel are often misunderstood.

The good thing is that all Evos – and the later models in particular – are very well catered for by the standard equipment, so unless you really are a ragged-edge track hero, you'll be just fine on the standard stuff. For early cars that have begun to feel a bit less than perfect, though, there are a few ways to lift things back to where they were, and beyond.

If you decide to give your Evo a suspension makeover there are a few ways to go about it. The easiest and least expensive is just to fit an uprated/lowered spring kit, which will work in conjunction with your original dampers. Fitting shouldn't be too difficult, but there are safety issues when altering a vital part of your car's chassis like this, so be sure you know what you're doing, or leave it to a professional.

If you do choose the spring-only option, you should know that your dampers won't be too pleased. Controlling a stiffer spring is a tougher job for them to do, so expect them to last up to a third less than they would normally. And if they're already a bit tired, you could finish them off pretty quickly.

Spring-only choices are between linear and progressive rate coils; and then there's the ride height to consider. A progressive-rate spring can give a slightly better ride under normal road conditions, and then it stiffens up as the loading increases. A linear-rate spring stays the same, so expect it to be stiffer all the time. As for ride height, going lower than 25–30mm (1.0–1.2in) is a bad idea because you should really have a shorter damper to go with the new spring. Going lower than that will also wreck the finely tuned factory settings, so unless you're only going to pose in the car and rip it up round town, don't drop it into the weeds.

The better option is to get a matched damper-and-spring combination, where the suspension company's engineers have evaluated what works best on your model of Evo and put together a pair of components that will work well together. Then you

DID YOU KNOW?

If you swap your wheels over make sure you torque your wheelnuts up at the time, and also check them again about 100 miles (160km) later. You don't want to be losing any nuts on the way home from a track day, do you?

Right: Adjustable mountings like these Tein units allow the camber to be altered to change the car's turn-in and steering characteristics. This means a road car can be set up for good stability and to be very solid on the road, while a track car can be made to turn into a corner much more easily, but be more nervous in a straight line.

Below: Trick coil-over dampers allow the car's ride height to be adjusted to suit track or road use. Be aware that they can be very stiff and too harsh for road use unless you're a diehard speed freak.

should get a reasonable ride round town, and properly controlled suspension when you're out on the twisties. And because the two things are properly matched, the dampers shouldn't throw in the towel too early.

For track-day heroes, the top choice is the fully-adjustable coil-over kit. This consists of a damper with a spring fitted to it on an adjustable-collar system that allows the ride height to be raised and lowered as necessary. The damper usually has adjustable damping characteristics too, so that the best performance can be dialled in and altered as tracks or conditions change. These kits often come with adjustable top-mounts that allow the camber angle to be altered. Getting the most from an arrangement like this is probably outside the ability of the majority of drivers, but the specialist who sells the gear should be able to advise on how to set it up for decent performance. Then as you get used to it you can

Above: Uprated anti-roll bars are also well worth considering when upgrading an Evo's sussies.

Above right: Strut braces don't have to be steel or ali; you can get them in carbon fibre if you'd really like.

Right: A three-point strut brace is the best brace to fit to an Evo if it hasn't already had one added. The brace firms up the front end, making steering more accurate and helping everything remain unflustered when the car is working hard. Bolting to the strut towers and the middle of the bulkhead, they pass stresses through to the car body rather than just straight across to the other suspension mount.

Adding extra suspension bracing can be very worthwhile, and something like this lower front brace can firm up the steering response nicely.

A rear strut brace is also worth investing in if you drive the car like it was meant to be driven.

tweak the various parameters and get closer to ideal settings for your car, your driving style, and the track you're on.

Another variable to consider on an Evo is some form of suspension bracing if your car hasn't either got it from the factory or had after-market braces added by a previous owner. Front upper strut braces are a great idea and will tighten up the steering feel no end if there isn't one on there already. Lower front braces are worthwhile too, as they improve the handling without making the car an ultra-stiff pig on regular roads. Rear braces also help, particularly the one that joins the upper suspension pickups together. It only eats a little boot space, and it's definitely

DID YOU KNOW?

If you're going to fit adjustable-height coil-overs, make sure you keep the adjuster threads clean. It's not uncommon for people to try and adjust the ride height only to find that the spring collar has corroded solid after a surprisingly short period of time.

Fitting different rims is a great idea, but make sure you don't add anything that's heavier than the original equipment or you could upset the handling and suspension set-up on the car.

worth the sacrifice. At both ends of the car it's best to go for triangulated braces that join the suspension towers to the bodywork at a third point, as these are much more rigid.

Regardless of which mods you choose, you must have the vehicle's suspension geometry checked and reset to compensate for the any changes you've made, to restore the car's handling and steering. If you don't you could end up with a car that steers badly, tramlines all over the road, doesn't want to go round corners properly, and chomps its way through tyres in a few hundred miles. Get it set up correctly and you'll relish every twist on your favourite road.

Wheels and tyres

The final link in the performance chain is your Evo's wheels and tyres. To some people, the main thing about wheels and tyres is to get something that looks good and lasts for miles, but there's a lot more to choosing

Well, the Evo always was a rally car, so why not go for the rally look?

and uprating them than that. After all, you can have a tremendously grunty motor, the most sophisticated suspension, and the most powerful brakes available, but if your car doesn't grip the road, it's all pretty useless.

Let's assume you're looking for an improvement in handling and roadholding, rather than just wanting the biggest things you can physically fit under the arches and sod the way the car drives. There are a few considerations to take into account before you stump up your hard-earned. Let's take wheels first.

Almost any Evo apart from the original – although they can go a little bigger if you're careful – will take a bigger wheel than is standard; it's just a question of how far you can or should go. For argument's sake, if you're running an Evo II on 15-inchers, 16s will generally be no problem, and most 17s would probably go on as well. Any bigger than that and you start to run the risk of ruining the handling, as well as the wheel and tyre being just too big for the wheel arch.

The main things to check are that the offset of the wheel is correct, and that the bigger rim doesn't catch any bodywork, suspension, or braking components. The offset refers to the distance from the centreline of the rim to the mounting face of the wheel, and this distance is crucial for maintaining correct steering characteristics and stopping premature tyre wear. As for the physical clearance, get specialist advice on what will fit your car – either from a wheel store or from someone who knows your model of Evo well – to make sure you get the right size that will clear things like your chunky calipers.

As well as the size and fit aspects, wheel material is also worth thinking about. Although most people probably think all alloy wheels are the same, there's plenty of diversity out there. Wheels basically come in three types – cast alloy, three-piece, and forged alloy. Cast wheels are split by the casting method, which is either gravity-fed or low-pressure. The best one is low-pressure, where the molten alloy is pumped into the mould, and as it cools down and voids begin to form more alloy is pumped in to fill the holes.

Three-piece wheels consist of a cast alloy centre with a spun aluminium rim. The lightness of the rim is usually counteracted by the weight of the centre piece, so don't expect much of a weight saving by going for expensive split rims. If you do want to use some of this type, go for the ones with plenty of bolts. The more fastenings there are holding the pieces together, the stronger the wheel will be, and the less it will leak.

The strongest and lightest wheel type is the forged aluminium. After squashing a solid block of alloy into a round shape, the actual wheel is machined from the block. This is an expensive method of wheel manufacture because there's so much wastage per wheel, but it does give the best results.

As for materials, almost every alloy wheel around is made from aluminium alloy. This is another minefield, though, because there are different grades of alloy. Virgin alloy is very pure and hasn't been through any other processes before it gets squashed or cast.

Secondary alloy, and those beyond, are recycled alloys that have been through some form of previous use and have then been reclaimed to be used again. While this sounds like a very 'green' thing to do, the secondary alloy can pick up impurities and end up not being as strong as virgin material.

Obviously, all these wheel types should pass various tests and be up to the job of carrying you safely, but if you are more demanding and use your car hard you need to look for the best wheel you can get. Something with a motorsport pedigree is going to be better than a purely cosmetic jobbie, but the best way to find out is to ask the salesman exactly what type of manufacture was used in the production of your chosen wheel, and see what he says. If he fills you with confidence, go ahead. If he waffles a lot, go somewhere else.

Once you've narrowed down your wheel choice, all you have to do is pick the rubber to wrap them in, which leads us neatly to tyres. If we're taking it as read that any wheel swap will increase the rim size by an inch or two, obviously the tyres that were originally fitted are no use on the new ones. That means you have to choose a tyre that not only fits the wheel, but fits under the wheel arch and can also cope with the loads you're about to inflict upon it.

Size-wise, the main point is that you keep the overall diameter as close to the original tyre as possible. The European Tyre and Rim Technical Organisation (ETRTO) advise that the new diameter is within +2 to –3 per cent of the manufacturer-fitted rubber to keep everything safe and accurate. So, if you had a 205/55/16 with a diameter of 633mm, something like a 225/45/17 is pretty close at 636mm. This should also keep your speedo more or less accurate.

Getting the right size is only half the battle though. You have to be sure that the tyre's speed and load rating are suited to your car. There's no point in fitting some cool low-profile rubber if it can't take the weight of your Evo when it's bogged down with the family and the holiday luggage. OK, family and luggage is unlikely, but you don't want a tyre to go pop as you exit a fast corner and need all the grip your car's got. The load code is marked on the side of the tyre along with the speed rating, so you can make sure that your new rubber is as strong as the original. Like the size conversion tables or calculators, this information is available on most tyre websites, so you can get the info direct.

If you're buying your wheels and tyres as a package

Clear rear lamp units change the rear end look without going over the top. Mitsubishi must like them because the Evo VIII has them from new.

from one of the many suppliers that are out there, you can check all these details with the sales staff, and it should give you an idea of how switched on they are. At least by buying a package you are spared the job of getting the tyres fitted to the wheels by someone else, which can be a mission in itself, particularly if you've gone for something very large and low profile. It's not that they can't physically fit the tyre – most tyre bays

Although we haven't shown much in the way of bodykits for Evos, there are a few bits out there and this aggressive front end moulding certainly looks the part.

can handle a 17in or 18in wheel without any problems – but some big chains say they can't fit tyres supplied by someone else because their insurance will be void. And while we're talking about fitting, have steel valves in preference to rubber ones, because steelies are more durable at 'high' speeds.

Once you're rolling on your new rubber, you'll almost certainly notice a new firmness to the ride, particularly if you've gone up a couple of inches in rim size on an earlier Evo. This is because a low-profile sidewall has less flex than a high-profile, so more road shocks are transmitted through to the suspension. If you've also lowered and stiffened the car, you might find the ride becomes actively uncomfortable on bad roads where you had no problems before.

Unfortunately, you can't really get round this problem, unless you go back to the suspension manufacturer and try and get some custom springs and dampers made. Mitsubishi can design a car to run on low profile rubber and alter the suspension to suit, but if you're doing the modifications you'll probably have to live with the bumpier ride. The better handling – as long

as you haven't gone too radical with the new wheel/tyre combo – should be worth it on track days and smooth roads, though.

One other consideration is the tyre pressure. Bigger tyres with shorter sidewalls need to run a higher pressure than the higher-profile tyres they replace. The general rule is to increase pressure by two psi for every extra inch of rim size. This helps the stiffer sidewalls to carry the loadings better, rather than letting them flex around too much and possibly damage the carcass.

And make sure you check the pressures regularly, because that stiff low-profile sidewall will disguise when the tyre is under-inflated, and that can lead to premature failure. Normally that's at three in the morning, on a rainy motorway, when you haven't got a spare that'll fit. So look after your tyres, and they'll look after you.

Chapter Eleven

Track days and holidays

Even though we're nearly at the end of the book, I suppose it's time for a bit of a reality check. Don't worry, it won't be a very long one, but if we don't mention this subject somewhere we'll have the Bland Police, the State Nannies and the Tedium Agency after us all. OK, that should have offended them enough.

The question that all the do-gooders would like to ask is where are you going to use the prodigious performance potential of an Evo – any Evo – to the full? Anyone who answered 'Peckham High Street' should probably leave the room now. With a top speed on the naughty side of 150mph (240kph), and acceleration quicker than most road users can begin to comprehend, giving an Evo its head on regular roads can be a bit hairy.

You need to be sensible when dealing with a weapon like an Evo, and the obvious answer to the question is to get off the public highway and find a place where you know there won't be anything nasty waiting round the bend. Like a tractor turning slowly into a field, or a coachload of grannies crossing the road on their way to a nice clotted cream tea. This means you could start entering competition, but this brings with it lots of extra expense and you'll end up with a car that – if it's tweaked enough to be competitive – will be too radical for street use.

The other alternative is to get yourself booked on to some of the many track days that are being run for anyone who wants to feel like a racer without the additional complications that racing brings. Then you'll be able to go as quickly as you feel comfortable, and you'll probably be able to get some on-track tuition to help you drive the car better.

Most track days are run by organisations which realise that there'll be several different levels of punter out there, so they are segregated into groups based on experience. That helps the circuit virgins to get a feel for what they're trying to do without being buzzed and upset by the faster drivers. Conversely, it lets the more experienced get to the ragged edge without having to take avoiding action at every apex as a new driver wobbles back onto the racing line and directly into the path of a quicker car.

Each day will be broken down into short sessions of around 20 minutes, and you can lap as many times as you can manage in that time. While 20 minutes might not sound a long time, once you've been concentrating hard for that length of time you'll probably be glad to get into the pits and cool down, and your car certainly will. If you start to get too tired to focus totally on what you're doing, you'll be closer to losing concentration and possibly having an accident. At most track days that would mean being sent home early, and if you have a bad smash you might shut the circuit for everyone else. Guess how popular you'd be then.

The on-track tuition can be incredibly useful. Having a seasoned racer sitting next to you pointing out the right lines, braking points, and where to turn into a corner helps you to get it right without having to experiment. After all, if you throw a shedload of cash at buying a car, and then spend more on tweaking it up to make it a real tarmac terrorist, you should also do something about the nut behind the wheel. And that's you. A few laps spent with someone who really knows his or her way around the circuit will make you safer *and* quicker.

Of course, the sort of use your Evo will get on the track is much harder than on the road, so you have to make sure absolutely everything about your car is up to spec before you get on circuit. Tyres and brakes can last a shockingly short period of time, especially if you

Above: Happy days. A country road, an Evo and a tankful of super unleaded. Let's go looking for motorbikes to chase...

Below: Get along to some car shows and you're bound to meet the nice people from the Mitsubishi Lancer Register. Join up and get the club benefits.

really get stuck in. We've seen people reduce tyres to threadbare covers with the metal showing, and watched others fitting new brake pads between sessions because the last lot have worn right down in a few outings.

It's also worth doing an oil and filter swap before the day so that you've got clean, fresh oil looking after your engine. On something like an Evo it's also a good idea to change the transmission fluids, because the stresses of high-intensity track work soon degrade oil and impair its ability to protect the gearbox and diffs. It might sound like an expensive routine to have to go through for a few laps round a circuit, but it's worth doing to keep your Evo in top condition.

One check that will be done at most venues is a noise test, to make sure your car isn't going to be too upsetting to the circuit's neighbours. If you've just fitted a big turbo with race wastegate that dumps exhaust direct to atmosphere through a few inches of open pipe, you might not be allowed on track.

To digress a moment, I can't understand why a race circuit has to bow to pressure brought on it by the people who moved into houses next door, but it seems that most racetracks can only be really noisy for a few days of the year, so track days have to be fairly quiet. I mean, what do you expect if you bought a house on the approach road to Castle Combe or Oulton Park? The clue is in the name 'racetrack'. Some people! If they want quiet, they should move somewhere else. Sorry, rant over.

Apart from making sure the car is up to the strain you're about to throw at it, you'll only need the minimum of other goodies before you can get out there and show everyone you really could have taken on Michael Schumacher, you just didn't get the same breaks he did. Most organisers will ask to see a driving licence to prove you know the brake from the accelerator, and you'll need full coverage clothing and an approved crash helmet.

The clothing just means you can't do laps in shorts and a tee-shirt, but jeans and a long-sleeve shirt are fine. There's no need to go for a full-on three-layer Nomex driving suit. In fact, turn up at a track day wearing one of those and you'd better be bloody good or you'll be hearing the laughter of the other drivers and the spectators even above the screaming of your engine...

As for the crash helmet, you could use one of those provided on the day, but you're much better getting your own and then you can make sure it fits your head

On the rolling road this exhaust manifold glows cherry red, and then goes on to bright orange as the revs rise.

properly. And that way you won't end up putting on a lid that's wet and clammy with someone else's perspiration either, which is always a bit off-putting.

Straight-lining it

If the thought of going round and round a race circuit isn't your thing, maybe you could have a go at drag racing. The Evo puts all its power down so well it can embarrass most other supposedly hot cars without yours even breaking sweat, and the tension of actually

Opposite: All sorts of Lancers on track.

Above: These Evos are passing the slower traffic – like this Porsche 911. Hah!

Below and right: As well as fitting go-faster bits there are plenty of shiny trinkets to dress up your engine bay if you'd like. Just don't spend all day polishing – get out and drive it.

racing head-to-head against someone else, and then beating them, feels great.

The only downside of drag racing is that it can be very hard on your car, particularly if you give it death on every race. The stress of dumping all the engine power down the drivetrain in a much more violent way than you would do anywhere else can break things, especially if you've had a bit of tuning done. Just be warned. Drag racing can be brilliant fun, but it can also be a real car killer.

Club details

As well as finding an outlet for the performance of the car, you should also think about joining the Mitsubishi Lancer Register, which is *the* club for Evo owners. Not only do they have a thriving online presence that can help you out with all manner of technical queries, they'll help you find parts, sell parts, buy a car, and generally

This is what happens if you get carried away with 700+bhp. The Norris Designs Evo VII went for a quick streak through the undergrowth at Castle Combe, but the superficial damage will probably polish out... And when you get your Evo on track, just make sure you drive within your capabilities, and enjoy.

keep in touch with other like-minded Evo nuts.

The club organises shows, rally days, rolling road shoot-outs, gets discounted track-day sessions, and has an insurance scheme to save you more money. For the cost of a good meal, membership is very worthwhile. You even get an MLR handbook, a quarterly mag, and a window decal. It will also put a long list of Mitsubishi specialists on your computer screen and you'll be able to ask the other members who gets the best recommendations for working on your own car. You can join online, so you don't even need an envelope or a stamp. How convenient is that?

Appendix A

Facts and figures

Mitsubishi Evolution I GSR

(RS differences in square brackets where applicable)

Chassis Code	CD9A-SNGF [SNDF]

Engine

Type	4G63 in-line 4-cylinder, 16-valve DOHC, turbo with intercooler and intercooler water spray
Fuel system	ECI-II MULTI (electronically controlled multi-point fuel injection)
Displacement	1,997cc
Bore/stroke	85.0/88.0mm
Compression ratio	8.5:1
Max output PS at rpm	250/6,000
Max torque lb ft at rpm	228/3,000
Emission control type	Catalytic converter
Maximum speed	112mph/180kph limited
Type of fuel	Super unleaded
Fuel tank capacity	50l (11gal)

Suspension and steering

Front axle	MacPherson strut
Rear axle	Multi-link with pillowball mountings
Brakes	Anti-lock Braking System
Front	Ventilated disc with 2-pot calipers
Rear	Solid disc with single-pot calipers
Steering	Power assisted, rack and pinion
Tyres	195/55R15
Wheels	15x6.5J alloy [15x7J steel]

Driveline

Type	Full-time 4WD with centre VCU (Viscous Coupling Unit)
Clutch	Single dry-plate with diaphragm spring

Transmission

Type	5-speed manual
Ratios	1st: 2.571
	2nd: 1.600
	3rd: 1.160
	4th: 0.862
	5th: 0.617
	Reverse: 3.166
Final gear ratio	5.433

Dimensions

Overall length	4,310mm (168.1in)
Overall width	1,695mm (66.1in)
Overall height	1,395mm (54.4in)
Wheelbase	2,500mm (97.5in)
Front track	1,450mm (56.6in)
Rear track	1,460mm (56.9in)
Min. ground clearance	150mm (5.8in)
Seating capacity	5
Vehicle weight	1,240kg (2,734lb) [1,170kg (2,580lb)]
Exterior colours	Pyrenees Black Pearl Grace Silver Metallic Carlton Red Saint Amour Green Metallic Scotia White [Scotia White, Grace Silver Metallic]

Mitsubishi Evolution II GSR

(RS differences in square brackets where applicable)

Chassis code	CE9A-SNGF [SNDF]

Engine

Type	4G63 in-line 4-cylinder, 16-valve DOHC, turbo with intercooler and intercooler water spray
Fuel system	ECI-II MULTI (electronically controlled multi-point fuel injection)

Displacement	1,997cc
Bore/stroke	85.0/88.0mm
Compression ratio	8.5:1
Max output PS at rpm	260/6,000
Max torque lb ft at rpm	228/3,000
Emission control type	Catalytic converter
Maximum speed	112mph/180kph limited
Type of fuel	Super unleaded
Fuel tank capacity	50l (11gal)

Suspension and steering

Front axle	MacPherson strut and forged lower arms
Rear axle	Multi-link with pillowball mountings
Brakes	Anti-lock Braking System
Front	Ventilated disc with 2-pot calipers
Rear	Solid disc with single-pot calipers
Steering	Power assisted, rack and pinion
Tyres	205/60R15
Wheels	15x6.5J alloy [15x7J steel]

Driveline

Type	Full-time 4WD with centre VCU
Clutch	Single dry-plate with diaphragm spring

Transmission

Type	5-speed manual
Ratios	1st: 2.750
	2nd: 1.684
	3rd: 1.160
	4th: 0.862
	5th: 0.617
	Reverse: 3.166
Final gear ratio	5.433

Dimensions

Overall length	4,310mm (168.1in)
Overall width	1,695mm (66.1in)
Overall height	1,420mm (55.4in)
Wheelbase	2,510mm (97.9in)
Front track	1,465mm (57.1in)
Rear track	1,470mm (57.3in)
Min ground clearance	170mm (6.6in)
Seating capacity	5
Vehicle weight	1,250kg (2,756lb) [1,180kg (2,602lb)]

Exterior colours	Pyrenees Black Pearl
	Queen's Silver Pearl
	Monaco Red
	Moonlight Blue Pearl
	Scotia White
	[Scotia White]

Mitsubishi Evolution III GSR

(RS differences in square brackets where applicable)

Chassis Code	CE9A-SNGF [SNDF]

Engine

Type	4G63 in-line 4-cylinder, 16-valve DOHC, turbo with intercooler and twin-jet intercooler water spray
Fuel system	ECI-II MULTI (electronically controlled multi-point fuel injection)
Displacement	1,997cc
Bore/stroke	85.0/88.0mm
Compression ratio	9.0:1
Max output PS at rpm	270/6,250
Max torque lb ft at rpm	228/3,000
Emission control type	Catalytic converter
Maximum speed	112mph/180kph limited
Type of fuel	Super unleaded
Fuel tank capacity	50l (11gal)

Suspension and steering

Front axle	MacPherson strut and forged lower arms
Rear axle	Multi-link with pillowball mountings
Brakes	Anti-lock Braking System
Front	Ventilated disc with 2-pot calipers
Rear	Solid disc with single-pot calipers
Steering	Power assisted, rack and pinion
Tyres	205/60R15
Wheels	15 x 6.5J alloy [15x7J steel]

Driveline

Type	Full-time 4WD with centre VCU
Clutch	Single dry-plate with diaphragm spring

Transmission

Type	5-speed manual
Ratios	1st: 2.750
	2nd: 1.684
	3rd: 1.160
	4th: 0.862
	5th: 0.617
	Reverse: 3.166
Final gear ratio	5.358

Dimensions

Overall length	4,310mm (168.1in)
Overall width	1,695mm (66.1in)
Overall height	1,420mm (55.4in)
Wheelbase	2,510mm (97.9in)
Front track	1,465mm (57.1in)
Rear track	1,470mm (57.3in)
Min ground clearance	175mm (6.8in)
Seating capacity	5
Vehicle weight	1,260kg (2,778lb) [1,190kg (2,624lb)]

Exterior colours	Pyrenees Black Pearl
	Queen's Silver Pearl
	Monaco Red
	Dandelion Yellow
	Scotia White
	[Scotia White]

Mitsubishi Evolution IV GSR

(RS differences in square brackets where applicable)

Chassis code	CN9A-SNGF [SNDF]

Engine

Type	4G63 in-line 4-cylinder, 16-valve DOHC, turbo with intercooler and twin-jet intercooler water spray
Fuel system	ECI-II MULTI (electronically controlled multi-point fuel injection)
Displacement	1,997cc
Bore/stroke	85.0/88.0mm
Compression ratio	8.8:1
Max output PS at rpm	280/6,500
Max torque lb ft at rpm	260/3,000
Emission control type	Catalytic converter
Maximum speed	112mph/180kph limited
Type of fuel	Super unleaded
Fuel tank capacity	50l (11gal)

Suspension and steering

Front axle	MacPherson strut and forged lower arms
Rear axle	Multi-link with pillowball mountings
Brakes	Anti-lock Braking System
Front	294mm ventilated disc with 2-pot calipers
Rear	284mm ventilated disc with single-pot calipers
Steering	Power assisted, rack and pinion
Tyres	205/50R16
Wheels	16x6.5J alloy [15x7J steel]

Driveline

Type	Full-time 4WD with centre VCU, Active Yaw Control rear differential
Clutch	Single dry-plate with diaphragm spring

Transmission

Type	5-speed manual
Ratios	1st: 2.785
	2nd: 1.950
	3rd: 1.407 [1.444]
	4th: 1.031 [1.096]
	5th: 0.761 [0.825]
	Reverse: 3.416
Final gear ratio	4.529 [High option 4.529; Low option 4.875]

Dimensions

Overall length	4,330mm (168.9in)
Overall width	1,690mm (65.9in)
Overall height	1,415mm (55.2in)
Wheelbase	2,510mm (97.9in)
Front track	1,470mm (57.3in)
Rear track	1,470mm (57.3in)
Min ground clearance	155mm (6.0in)
Seating capacity	5
Vehicle weight	1,350kg (2,977lb) [1,260kg (2,778lb)]

Exterior colours	Pyrenees Black Pearl
	Steel Silver Metallic
	Palma Red
	Icecelle Blue Pearl
	Scotia White
	[Scotia White]

Mitsubishi Evolution V GSR

(RS differences in square brackets where applicable)

Chassis code	CP9A-SNGF [SNDF]

Engine

Type	4G63 in-line 4-cylinder, 16-valve DOHC, turbo with intercooler and twin-jet intercooler water spray
Fuel system	ECI-II MULTI (electronically controlled multi-point fuel injection)
Displacement	1,997cc
Bore/stroke	85.0/88.0mm
Compression ratio	8.8:1
Max output PS at rpm	280/6,500
Max torque lb ft at rpm	274/3,000
Emission control type	Catalytic converter
Maximum speed	112mph/180kph limited
Type of fuel	Super unleaded
Fuel tank capacity	50l (11gal)

Suspension and steering

Front axle	MacPherson strut and forged lower arms
Rear axle	Multi-link with pillowball mountings
Brakes	Anti-lock Braking System
Front	Brembo 320mm ventilated disc with 4-pot calipers
Rear	Brembo 300mm ventilated disc with 2-pot calipers
Steering	Power assisted, rack and pinion
Tyres	225/45R17
Wheels	17x7.5J alloy [15x7J steel]

Driveline

Type	Full-time 4WD with centre VCU, Active Yaw Control rear differential
Clutch	Single dry-plate with diaphragm spring

Transmission

Type	5-speed manual
Ratios	1st: 2.785
	2nd: 1.950
	3rd: 1.407 [1.444]
	4th: 1.031 [1.096]
	5th: 0.761 [0.825]
	Reverse: 3.416
Final gear ratio	4.529 [High option 4.529; Low option 4.875]

Dimensions

Overall length	4,350mm (169.7in)
Overall width	1,770mm (69.0in)
Overall height	1,415mm (55.2in)
Wheelbase	2,510mm (97.9in)
Front track	1,510mm (58.9in) [1,495mm (58.3in)]
Rear track	1,505mm (58.7in) [1,490mm (58.1in)]
Min ground clearance	150mm (5.8in)
Seating capacity	5
Vehicle weight	1,360kg (2,999lb) [1,260kg (2,778lb)]
Exterior colours	Pyrenees Black Pearl
	Satellite Silver Metallic
	Palma Red
	Dandelion Yellow
	Scotia White
	[Scotia White]

Mitsubishi Evolution VI GSR

(RS differences in square brackets where applicable)

Chassis code	CP9A-SNGF [SNDF]

Engine	
Type	4G63 in-line 4-cylinder, 16-valve DOHC, turbo with intercooler and twin-jet intercooler water spray
Fuel system	ECI-II MULTI (electronically controlled multi-point fuel injection)
Displacement	1,997cc
Bore/stroke	85.0/88.0mm
Compression ratio	8.8:1
Max output PS at rpm	280/6,500
Max torque lb ft at rpm	274/3,000
Emission control type	Catalytic converter
Maximum speed	112mph/180kph limited
Type of fuel	Super unleaded
Fuel tank capacity	50l (11gal)

Suspension and steering

Front axle	MacPherson strut and forged lower arms
Rear axle	Multi-link with pillowball mountings
Brakes	Anti-lock Braking System
Front	Brembo 320mm ventilated disc with 4-pot calipers
Rear	Brembo 300mm ventilated disc with 2-pot calipers
Steering	Power assisted, rack and pinion
Tyres	225/45R17
Wheels	17x7.5J alloy [15x7J steel]

Driveline

Type	Full-time 4WD with centre VCU, Active Yaw Control rear differential
Clutch	Single dry-plate with diaphragm spring

Transmission

Type	5-speed manual
Ratios	1st: 2.785
	2nd: 1.950
	3rd: 1.407 [1.444]
	4th: 1.031 [1.096]
	5th: 0.761 [0.825]
	Reverse: 3.416
Final gear ratio	4.529 [High option 4.529; Low option 4.875]

Dimensions

Overall length	4,350mm (169.7in)
Overall width	1,770mm (69.0in)
Overall height	1,405mm (54.7in) [1,415mm (55.2in)]
Wheelbase	2,510mm (97.9in)
Front track	1,510mm (58.9in) [1,495mm (58.3in)]
Rear track	1,505mm (58.7in) [1,490mm (58.1in)]
Min ground clearance	140mm (5.5in) [150mm (5.8in)]
Seating capacity	5
Vehicle weight	1,360kg (2,999lb) [1,250kg (2,756lb)]

Exterior colours	Pyrenees Black Pearl
	Satellite Silver Metallic
	Lance Blue
	Icecelle Blue
	Scotia White
	[Scotia White]

Mitsubishi Evolution VI Tommi Makinen Edition

(RS differences in square brackets where applicable)

Chassis code	CP9A-SNGF (Special Colour Pack SNGF2) [SNDF]

Engine

Type	4G63 in-line 4-cylinder, 16-valve DOHC, turbo with intercooler and twin-jet intercooler water spray
Fuel system	ECI-II MULTI (electronically controlled multi-point fuel injection)
Displacement	1,997cc
Bore/stroke	85.0/88.0mm
Compression ratio	8.8:1
Max output PS at rpm	280/6,500
Max torque lb ft at rpm	274/3,000
Emission control type	Catalytic converter
Maximum speed	112mph/180kph limited
Type of fuel	Super unleaded
Fuel tank capacity	50l (11gal)

Suspension and steering

Front axle	MacPherson strut and forged lower arms
Rear axle	Multi-link with pillowball mountings
Brakes	Anti-lock Braking System
Front	Brembo 320mm ventilated disc with 4-pot calipers
Rear	Brembo 300mm ventilated disc with 2-pot calipers
Steering	Power assisted, rack and pinion
Tyres	225/45R17
Wheels	17x7.5J alloy [15x7J steel]

Driveline

Type	Full-time 4WD with centre VCU, Active Yaw Control rear differential
Clutch	Single dry-plate with diaphragm spring

Transmission

Type	5-speed manual
Ratios	1st: 2.785
	2nd: 1.950
	3rd: 1.407 [1.444]
	4th: 1.031 [1.096]
	5th: 0.761 [0.825]
	Reverse: 3.416
Final gear ratio	4.529 [High option 4.529; Low option 4.875)

Dimensions

Overall length	4,350mm (169.7in)
Overall width	1,770mm (69.0in)
Overall height	1,405mm (54.8in) [1,415mm (55.2in)]
Wheelbase	2,510mm (97.9in)
Front track	1,510mm (58.9in) [1,495mm (58.3in)]
Rear track	1,505mm (58.7in) [1,490mm (58.1in)]
Min ground clearance	140mm (5.5in) [150mm (5.8in)]
Seating capacity	5
Vehicle weight	1,360kg (2,999lb) [1,250kg (2,756lb)]
Exterior colours	Passion Red (with special colouring package)
	Pyrenees Black Pearl
	Satellite Silver Metallic
	Canal Blue
	Scotia White
	[Scotia White]

Mitsubishi Evolution VII GSR
(RS differences in square brackets where applicable)

Chassis code	CT9A-SNDFZ [SNGFZ]

Engine

Type	4G63 in-line 4-cylinder, 16-valve DOHC, turbo with intercooler and triple-jet intercooler water spray
Fuel system	ECI-II MULTI (electronically controlled multi-point fuel injection)
Displacement	1,997cc
Bore/stroke	85.0/88.0mm
Compression ratio	8.8:1

Max output PS at rpm	280/6,500
Max torque lb ft at rpm	282/3,500
Emission control type	Catalytic converter
Maximum speed	112mph/180kph limited (UK 157mph/253kph)
Type of fuel	Super unleaded
Fuel tank capacity	48l (10.5gal)

Suspension and steering

Front axle	MacPherson strut with inverted damper, stabiliser bar and forged aluminium lower arms
Rear axle	Multi-link with pillowball mountings, stabiliser bar and forged aluminium arms
Brakes	Sports ABS system
Front	Brembo 320mm ventilated disc with 4-pot calipers
Rear	Brembo 300mm ventilated disc with 2-pot calipers
Steering	Power assisted, rack and pinion
Tyres	235/45R17
Wheels	17x8JJ alloy [15x7J steel]

Driveline

Type	Full-time 4WD with ACD Active Centre Differential, Active Yaw Control rear differential
Clutch	Single dry-plate with diaphragm spring

Transmission

Type	5-speed manual
Ratios	1st: 2.928 [2.785]
	2nd: 1.950
	3rd: 1.407 [1.444]
	4th: 1.031 [1.096]
	5th: 0.720 [0.825]
	Reverse: 3.416
Final gear ratio	4.529

Dimensions

Overall length	4,455mm (173.7in)
Overall width	1,770mm (69.0in)
Overall height	1,450mm (56.6in)
Wheelbase	2,625mm (102.4in)
Front track	1,515mm (59.1in) [1,500mm (58.5in)]

Rear track	1,515mm (59.1in) [1,500mm (58.5in)]	Brakes	Sports ABS system

Rear track   1,515mm (59.1in) [1,500mm (58.5in)]

Min ground clearance   140mm (5.5in)

Seating capacity   5

Vehicle weight   1,400kg (3,087lb) [1,320kg (2,911lb)]

Exterior colours   Amethyst Black Pearl
Satellite Silver Metallic
French Blue
Palma Red
Eisen Grey
Dandelion Yellow
Scotia White
[Scotia White]

Mitsubishi Evolution VIII GSR
(RS differences in square brackets where applicable)

Chassis code   CT9A-SJGFZ, 6-speed GSR [SJDFZ, 6-speed RS; SNDFZ, 5-speed RS]

Engine

Type   4G63 in-line 4-cylinder, 16-valve DOHC, turbo with intercooler and triple-jet intercooler water spray

Fuel system   ECI-II MULTI (electronically controlled multi-point fuel injection)

Displacement   1,997cc

Bore/stroke   85.0/88.0mm

Compression ratio   8.8:1

Max output PS at rpm   280/6,500

Max torque lb ft at rpm   290/3,500

Emission control type   Catalytic converter

Maximum speed   112mph/180kph limited (UK models 157mph/253kph)

Type of fuel   Super unleaded

Fuel tank capacity   55l (12.1gal) [50l (11gal)]

Suspension and steering

Front axle   MacPherson strut with inverted damper, stabiliser bar and forged aluminium lower arms

Rear axle   Multi-link with pillowball mountings, stabiliser bar and forged aluminium arms

Brakes   Sports ABS system

Front   Brembo 320mm ventilated disc with 4-pot calipers

Rear   Brembo 300mm ventilated disc with 2-pot calipers

Steering   Power assisted, rack and pinion

Tyres   235/45R17

Wheels   17x8JJ alloy [15x7J steel]

Driveline

Type   Full-time 4WD with ACD Active Centre Differential, Super Active Yaw Control rear differential

Clutch   Single dry-plate with diaphragm spring

Transmission

Type   6-speed manual [5-speed manual]

Ratios   1st: 2.909 [2.785]
2nd: 1.944 [1.950]
3rd: 1.434 [1.444]
4th: 1.100 [1.096]
5th: 0.868 [0.825]
6th: 0.693
Reverse: 2.707 [3.416]

Final gear ratio   4.583 [4.529]

Dimensions

Overall length   4,490mm (175.1in)

Overall width   1,770mm (69.0in)

Overall height   1,450mm (56.6in)

Wheelbase   2,625mm (102.4in)

Front track   1,515mm (59.1in) [1,500mm (58.5in)]

Rear track   1,515mm (59.1in) [1,500mm (58.5in)]

Min ground clearance   140mm (5.5in)

Seating capacity   5

Vehicle weight   1,410kg (3,109lb) [1,320kg (2,911lb)]

Exterior colours   Amethyst Black Pearl
Cool Silver Metallic
Medium Purple Pearl
Palma Red
Dandelion Yellow
Scotia White
[Scotia White]

Specialists

If you've done the right thing and bought yourself a total weapon like a razor-sharp Evo, you'll want to keep it in good health, and possibly even tweak it a bit as well, right? So, listed here are a few contact names and numbers that should help you do just that. They've been picked because either I've personally dealt with them, they have a huge reputation in Mitsubishi tuning, or I've spoken to someone who has said nice things about them.

Obviously, this isn't a total *carte blanche* recommendation, so do the usual thing of ringing around to get advice and see who you get on with the best. Give your money to people who not only know what they're doing, but who let you know you're getting what you want. As for anyone who makes you feel that it's a privilege for you to speak to them, well...

Here's the list in purely alphabetical order.

Amber Performance, 713 Dunstable Road, Luton, Bedfordshire. 01582 572500. www.amber-performance.co.uk. sales@amber-performance.co.uk.

AWD Motorsport Engineering, 1 Inveralmond Road, Inveralmond Industrial Estate, Perth. 01738 633336. www.awdmotorsport.co.uk.

BTR Preparations, 55 Carrwood Road, Glasshoughton, Castleford, West Yorkshire. 01977 552348. www.btrprep.com. tim@btrprep.com.

Co-Ordsport Ltd, King Street, Dudley, West Midlands. 01785 220220. www.coordsport.co.uk. sales@coordsport.com.

DP Motorsport, 375 Old Liverpool Road, Sankey Bridges, Warrington, Cheshire. 01925 445174. www.dpmotorsport.com.

G-Force Motorsport Limited, 4–5 Edison Road, Rabans Lane Industrial Estate, Aylesbury, Buckinghamshire. 01296 434084. www.g-force-motorsport.co.uk. info@g-force-motorsport.co.uk.

Graham Goode Racing, Lutterworth Road, Leicester. 0116 244 0080. www.grahamgoode.com. sales@grahamgoode.com. tech@grahamgoode.com.

Grasshopper Pro-Sport, Unit C2, Moss Industrial Estate, St Helens Road, Leigh, Lancashire. 01942 671239. www.grasshopperprosport.co.uk. info@grasshopperprosport.co.uk.

Hyper Sports & Racing, Unit 1, Station Approach, Ladies Lane, Hindley, Near Wigan, Lancashire. 0845 2250111. www.hypersr.com. hypersportsracing@hotmail.com.

MA Developments, Maidenhead, Berkshire. 07768 356204. www.madevelopments.com. mark@madevelopments.com.

Nemesis Performance, Unit 7, School Farm, School Road, Langham, Colchester, Essex. 01206 273344. www.nemesisperformance.co.uk.

sales@nemesisperformance.co.uk.

Norris Designs, Unit 6c, Parklane Industrial Estate, Parklane, Corsham, Wiltshire. 01249 712024. www.norrisdesigns.com. sales@norrisdesigns.com.

Option Motorsport, Unit 3, West End Farm, Silverstone, Northants. 01327 858555. www.optionmotorsport.com. sales@optionmotorsport.com.

Power Engineering, The Power House, 8 Union Buildings, Wallingford Road, Uxbridge, Middlesex. 01895 255699. www.powerengineering.co.uk. sales@powerengineering.co.uk.

Racelogic, 5 Little Balmer, Buckingham Industrial Park, Buckingham. 01280 823803. racelogic.co.uk. sales@racelogic.co.uk.

RC Developments, Willows Garage, Runcorn Road, Barnton, Northwich, Cheshire. 01606 786706. www.rcdevelopments.com. info@rcdevelopments.com.

RS Autos. 01243 825573. www.rsautos.com

Spec-R, Unit G5, Avonside Enterprise Park, New Broughton Road, Melksham, Wiltshire. 01225 705507. www.spec-r.co.uk. enquiries@spec-r.co.uk.

Sumo Power, Kleer House, Sheerness Docks, Kent. 01795 668899. www.sumopower.com. info@sumopower.com.

TDI, 33 Trafalgar Business Centre, River Road, Barking, Essex. 0208 591 0442. www.tdi-plc.com.

Tuning Japanese, Unit A, 17 Maneway Business Units, Holder Road, Aldershot, Hants. 01252 328080. www.tuningjapanese.co.uk. tim@tuningjapanese.co.uk.

Wincanton Motor Services, Unit 10, Tythings Commercial Centre, Wincanton, Somerset. 01963 32999. www.wmstuning.com. sales@wmstuning.com.

Warrender Sports and Performance Cars Ltd, Willows Garage, Runcorn Road, Barnton, Northwich, Cheshire. 0845 330 8800. www.itsaveryfastworld.com. sales@warrender.co.uk.

Index